COLOR TEST PAGE

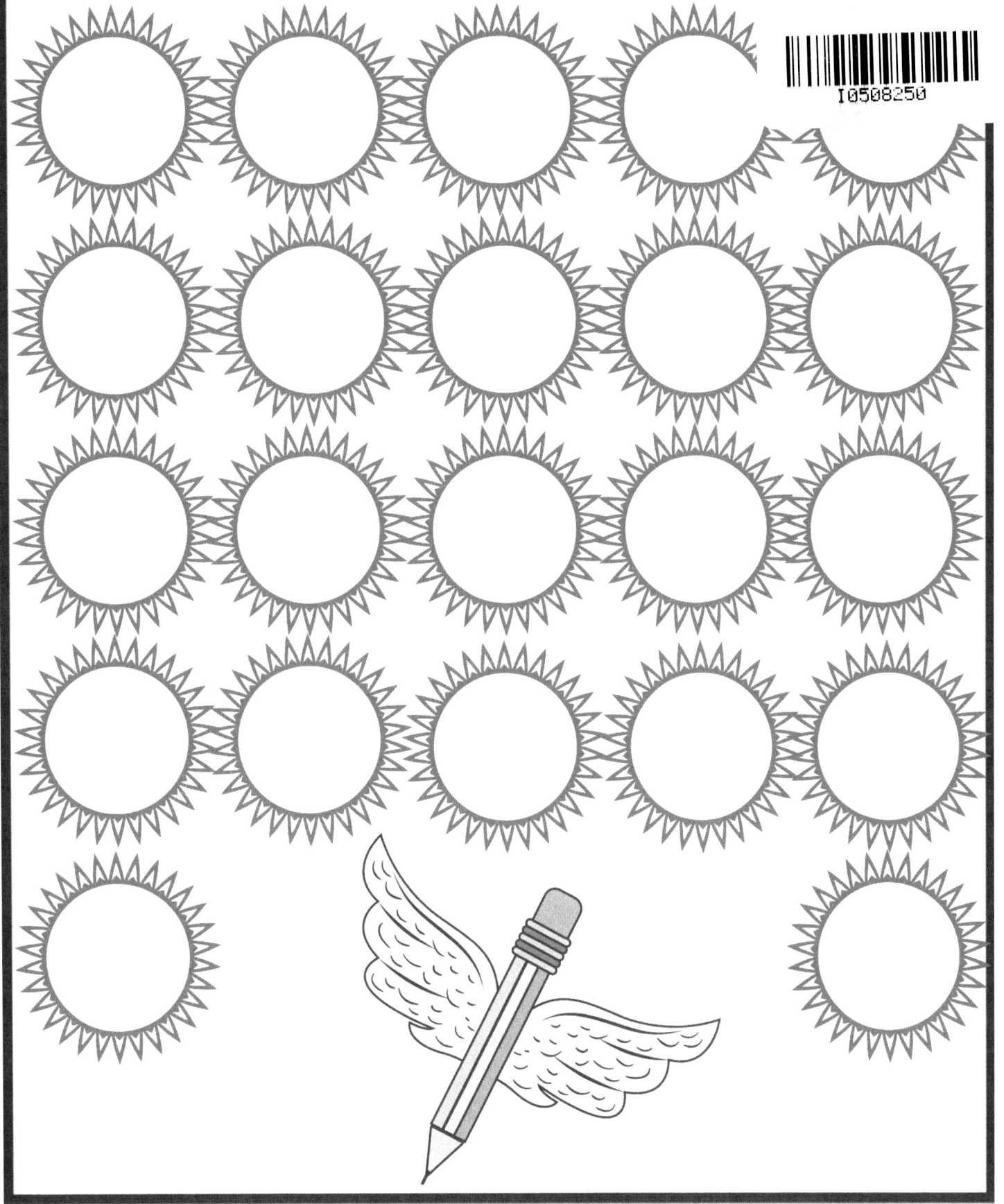

THIS BOOK BELONGS TO

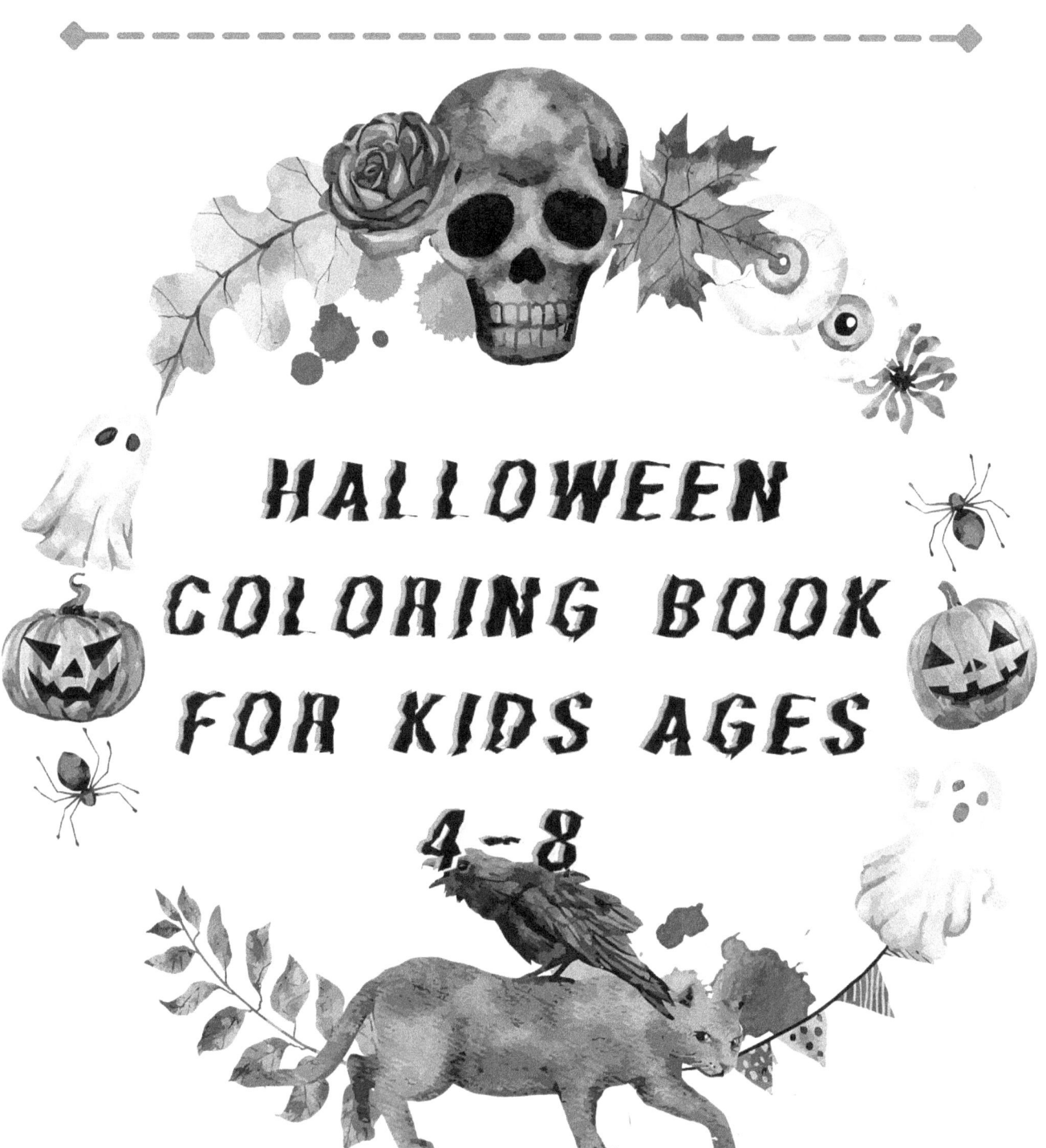

HALLOWEEN COLORING BOOK FOR KIDS AGES 4-8

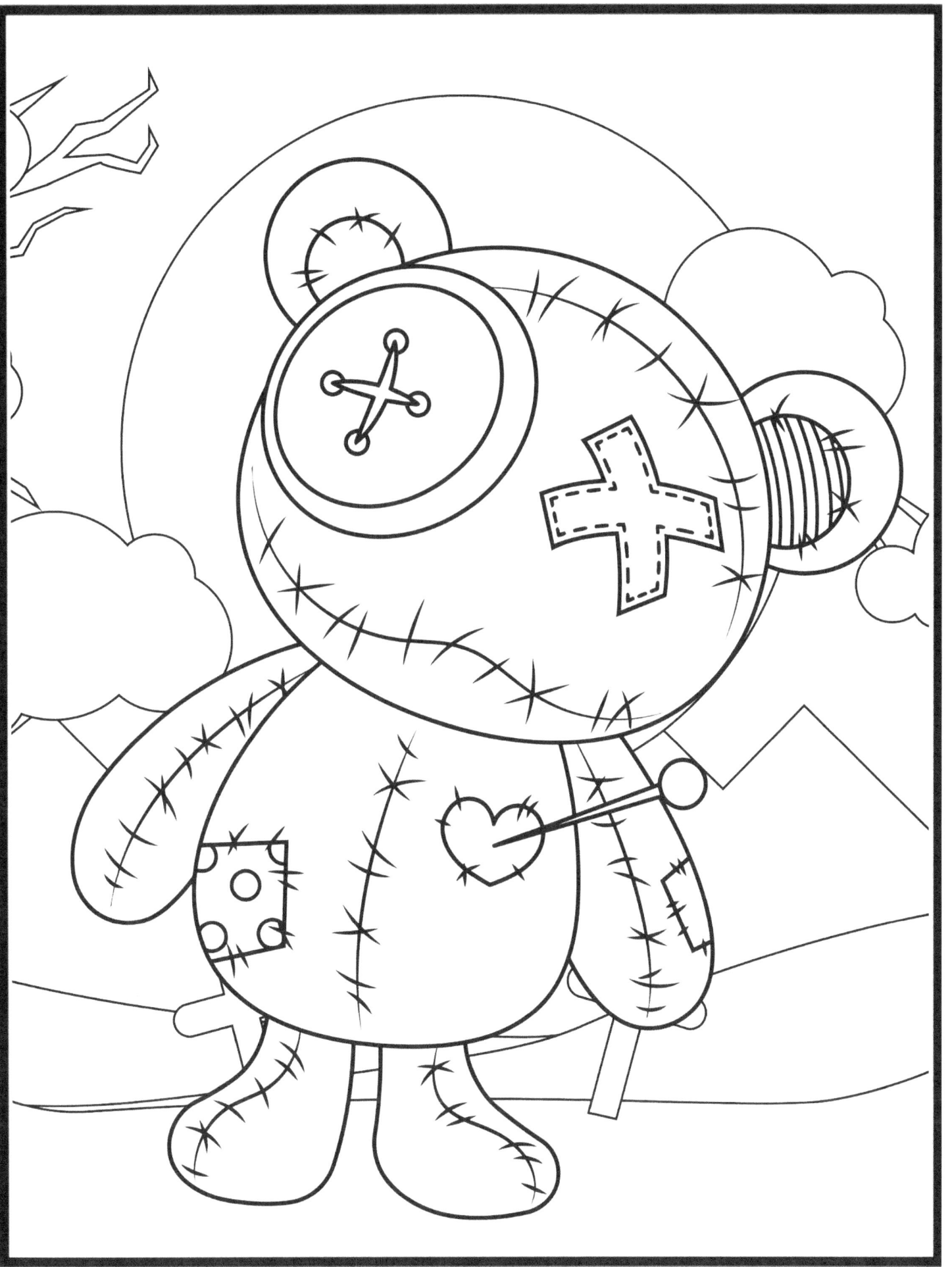

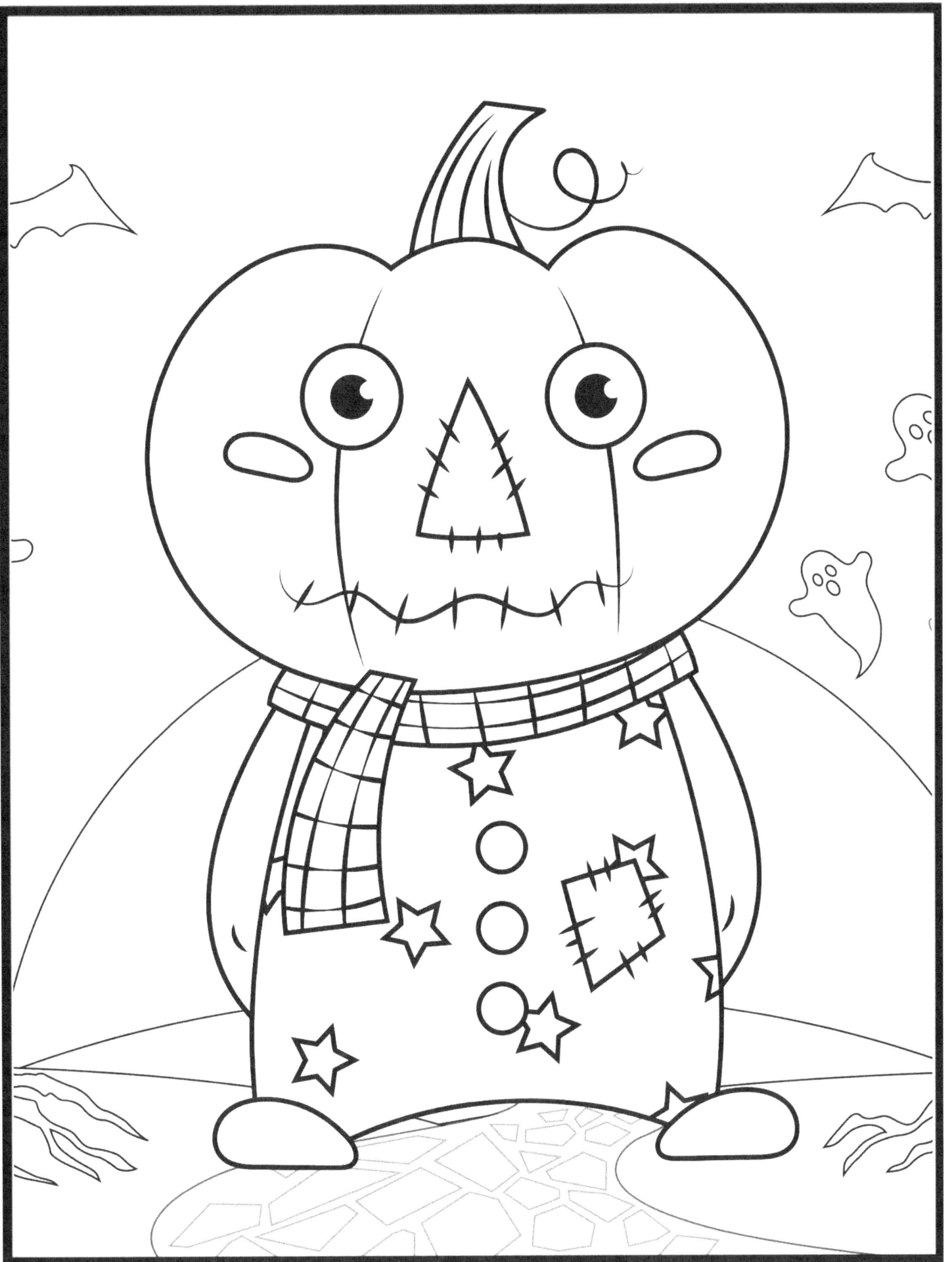

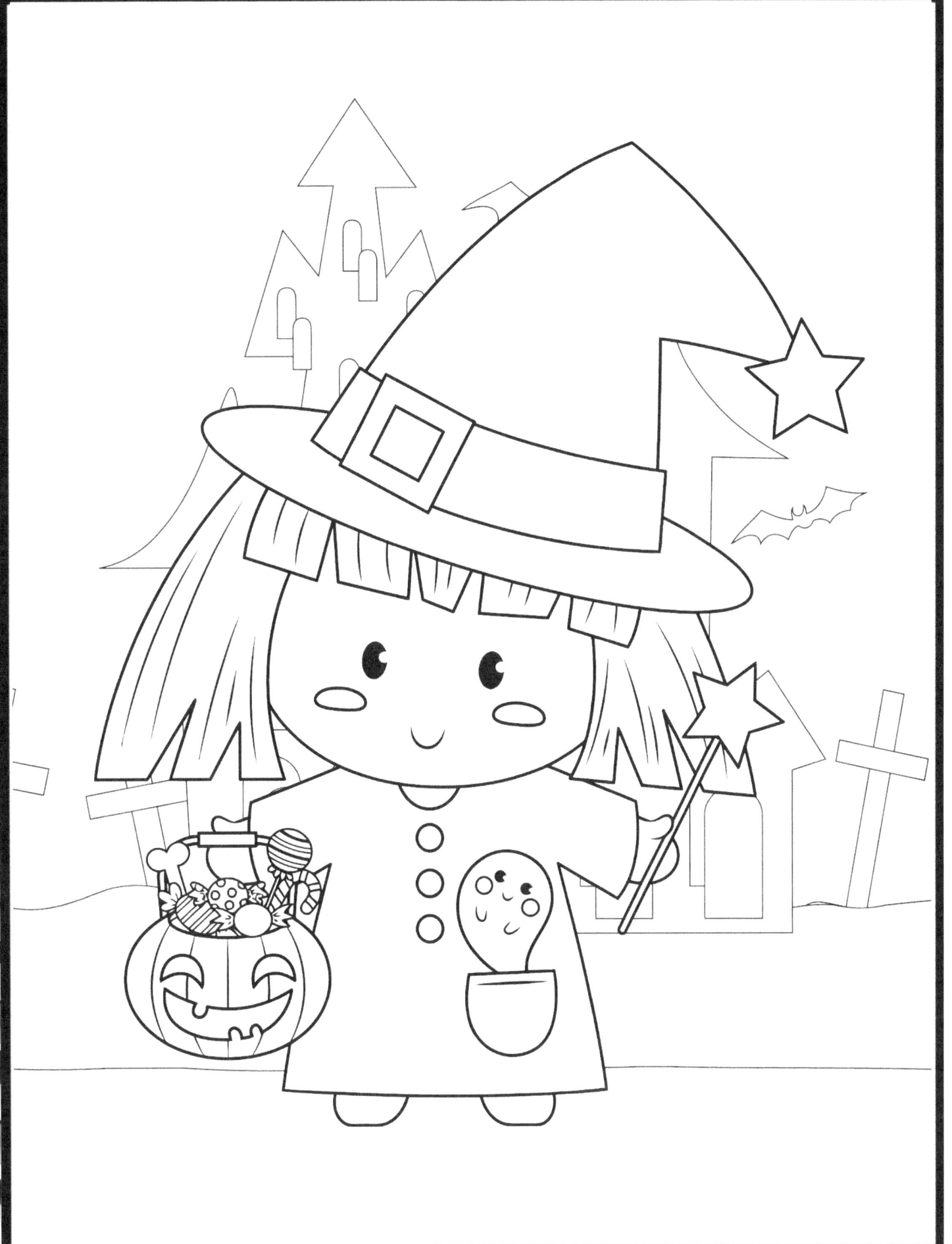

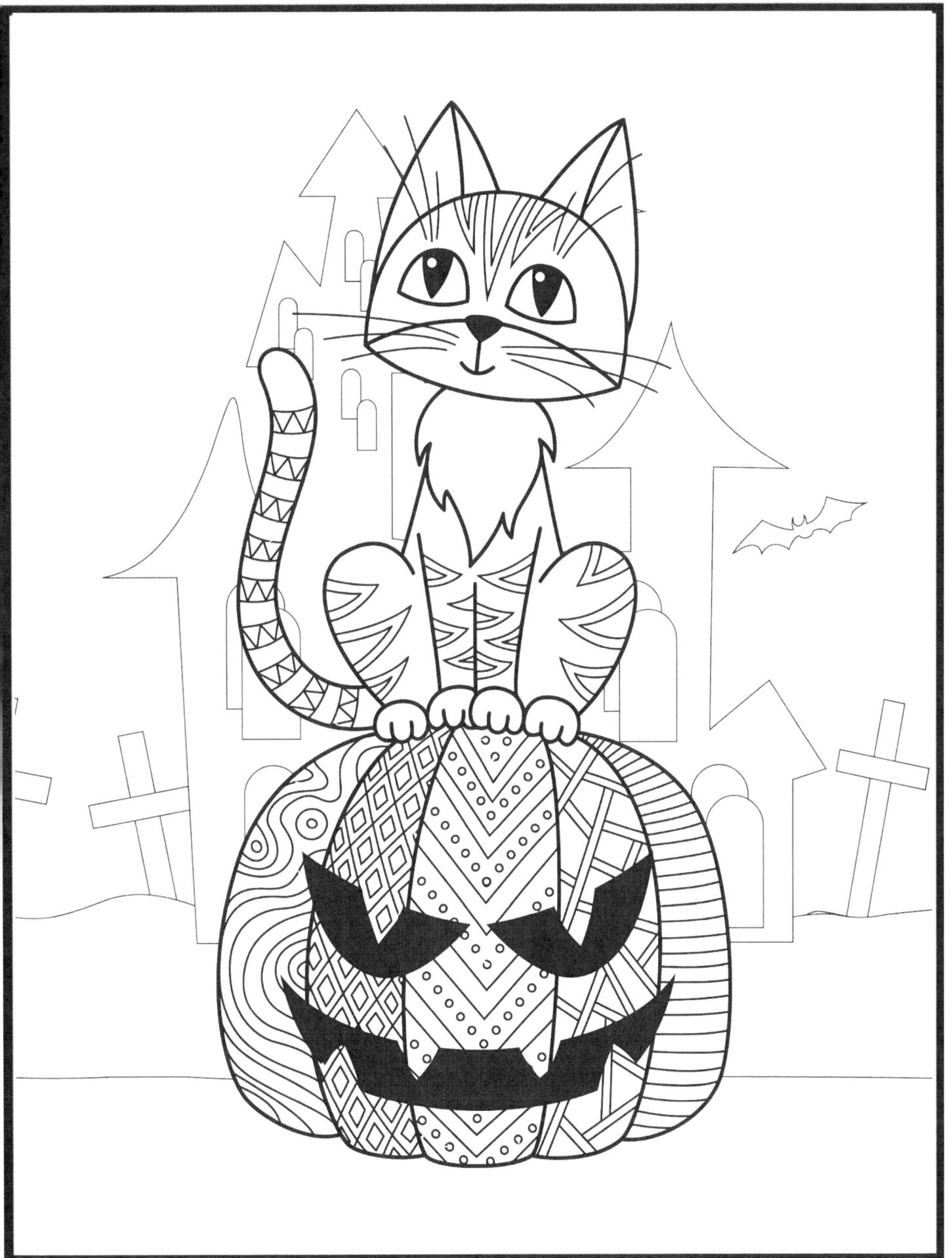

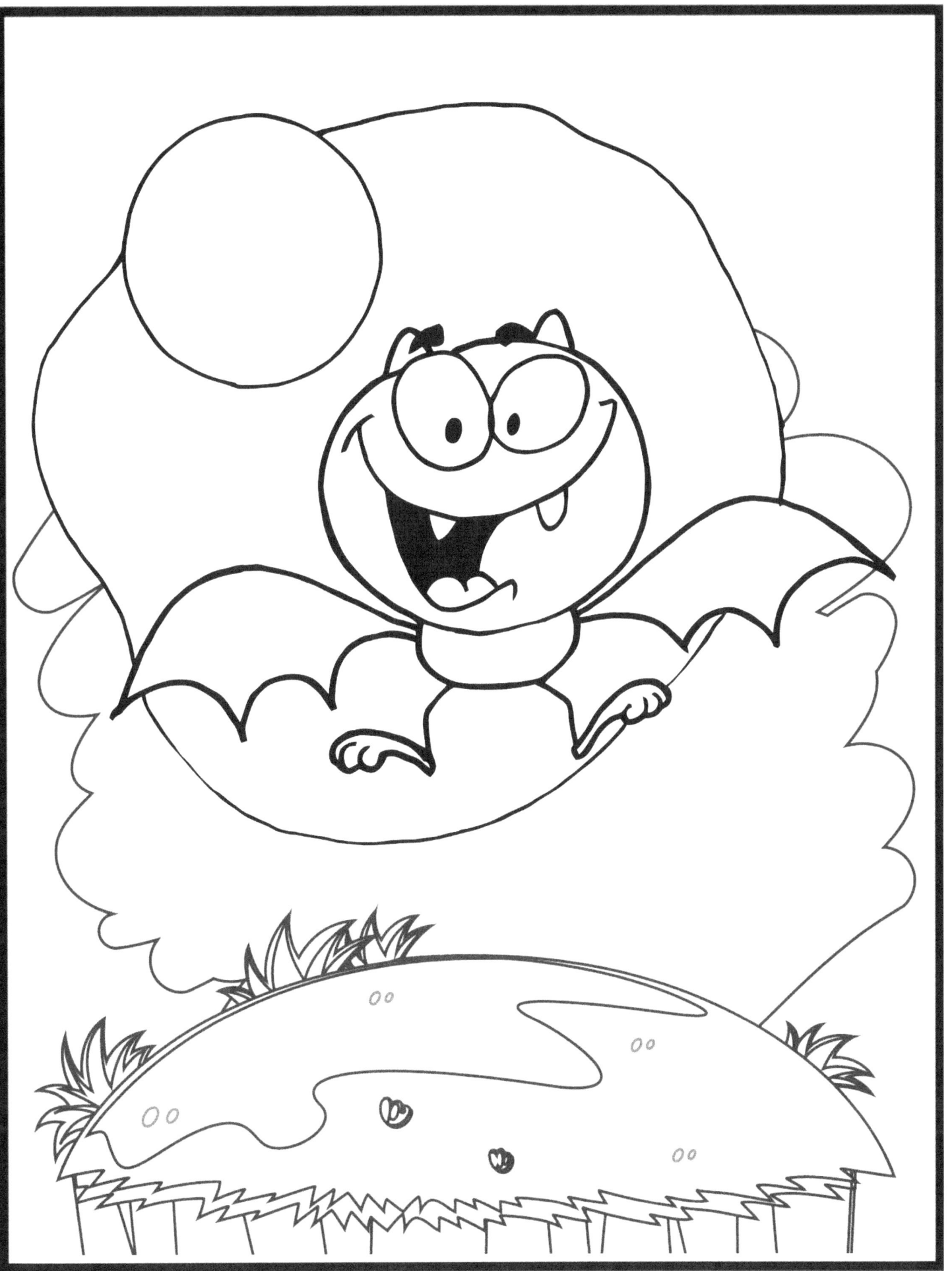

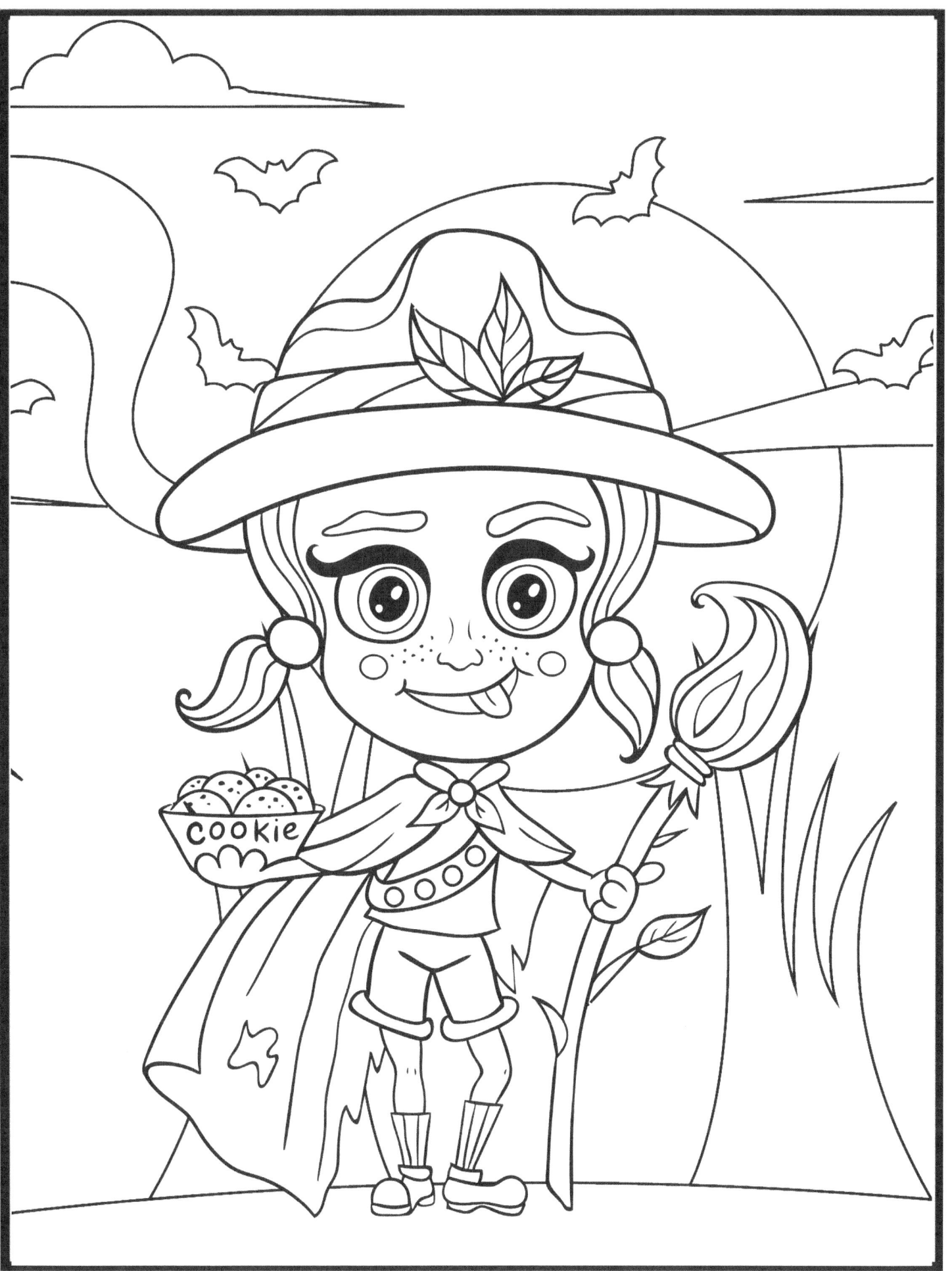

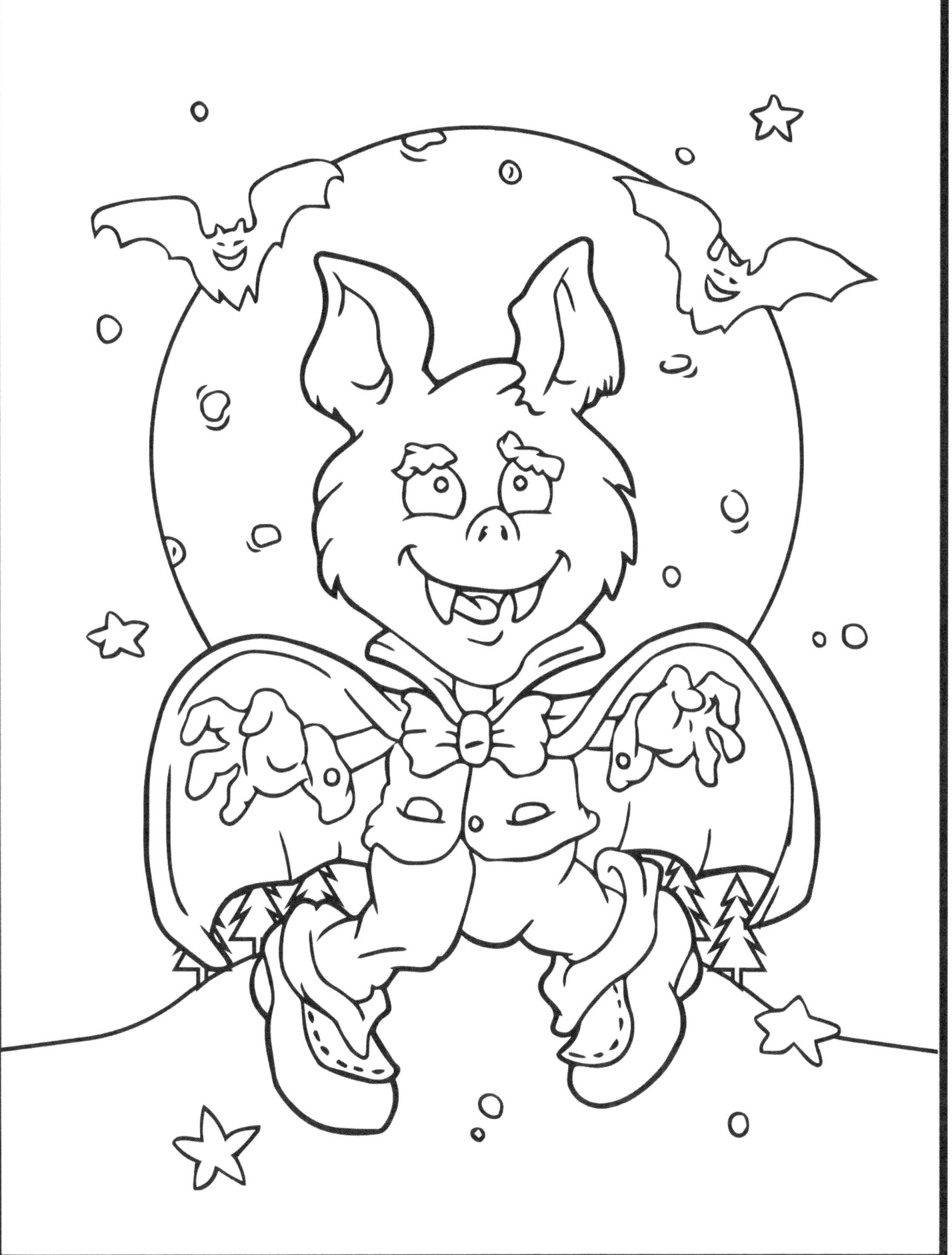

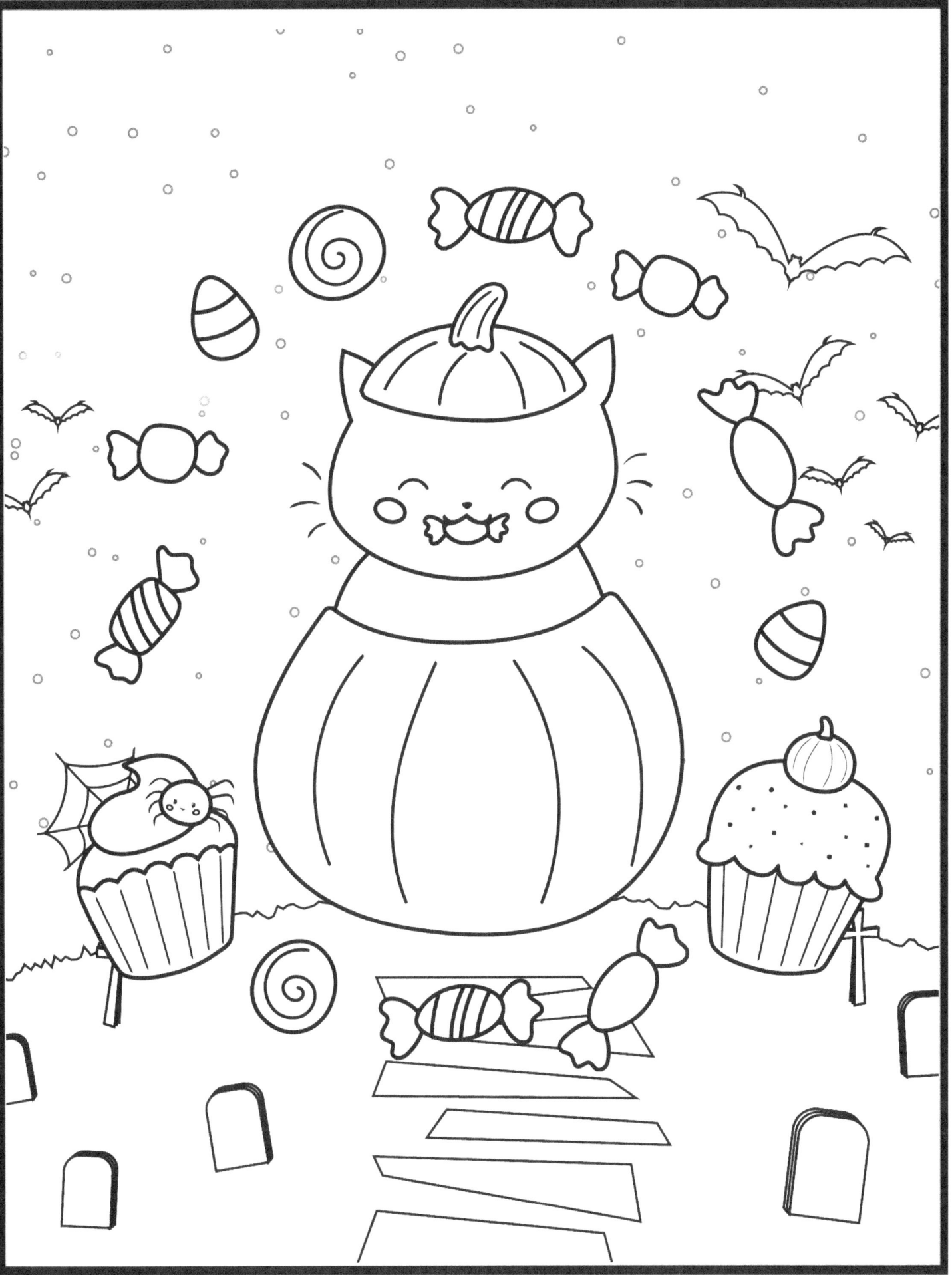

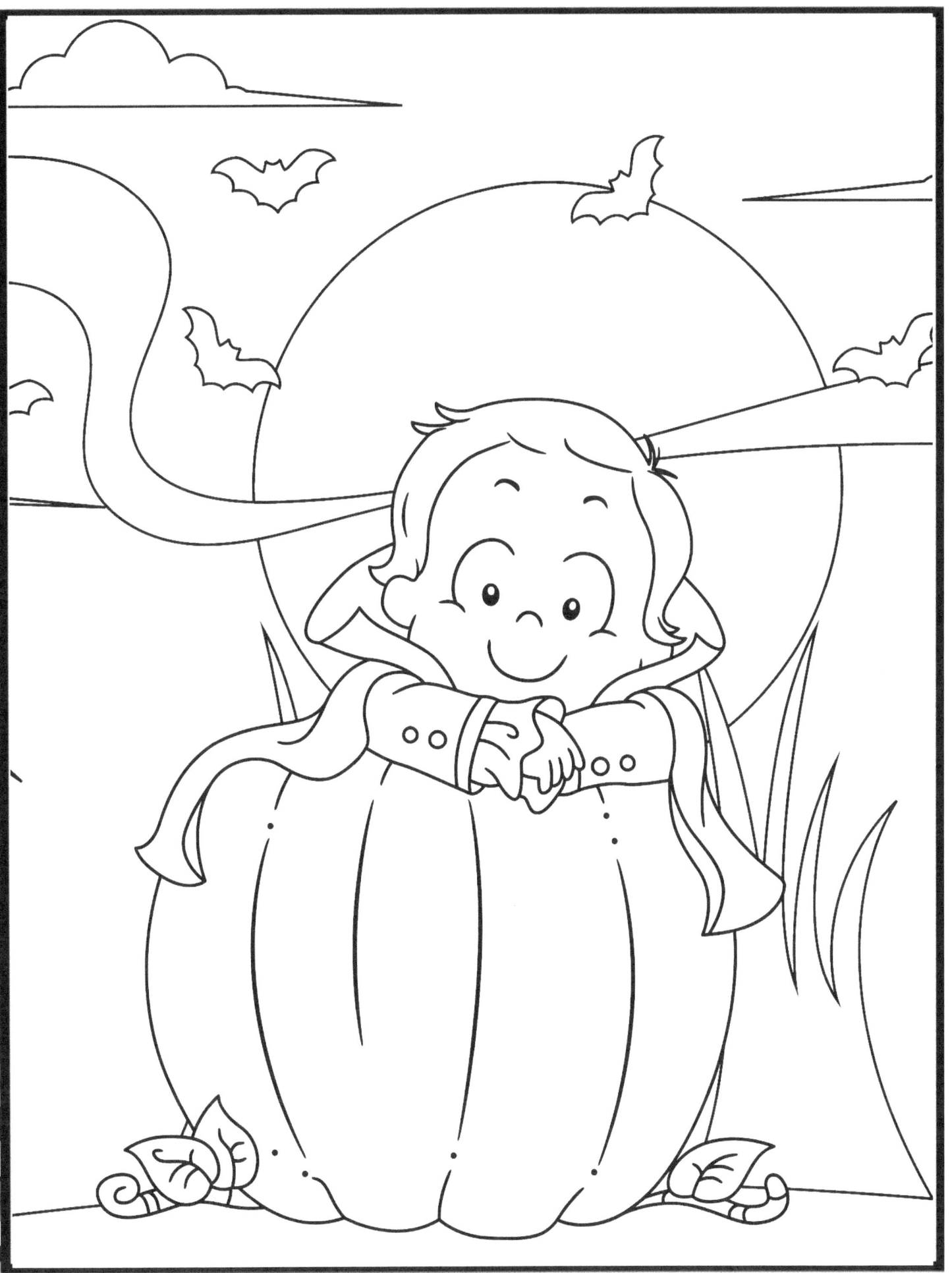

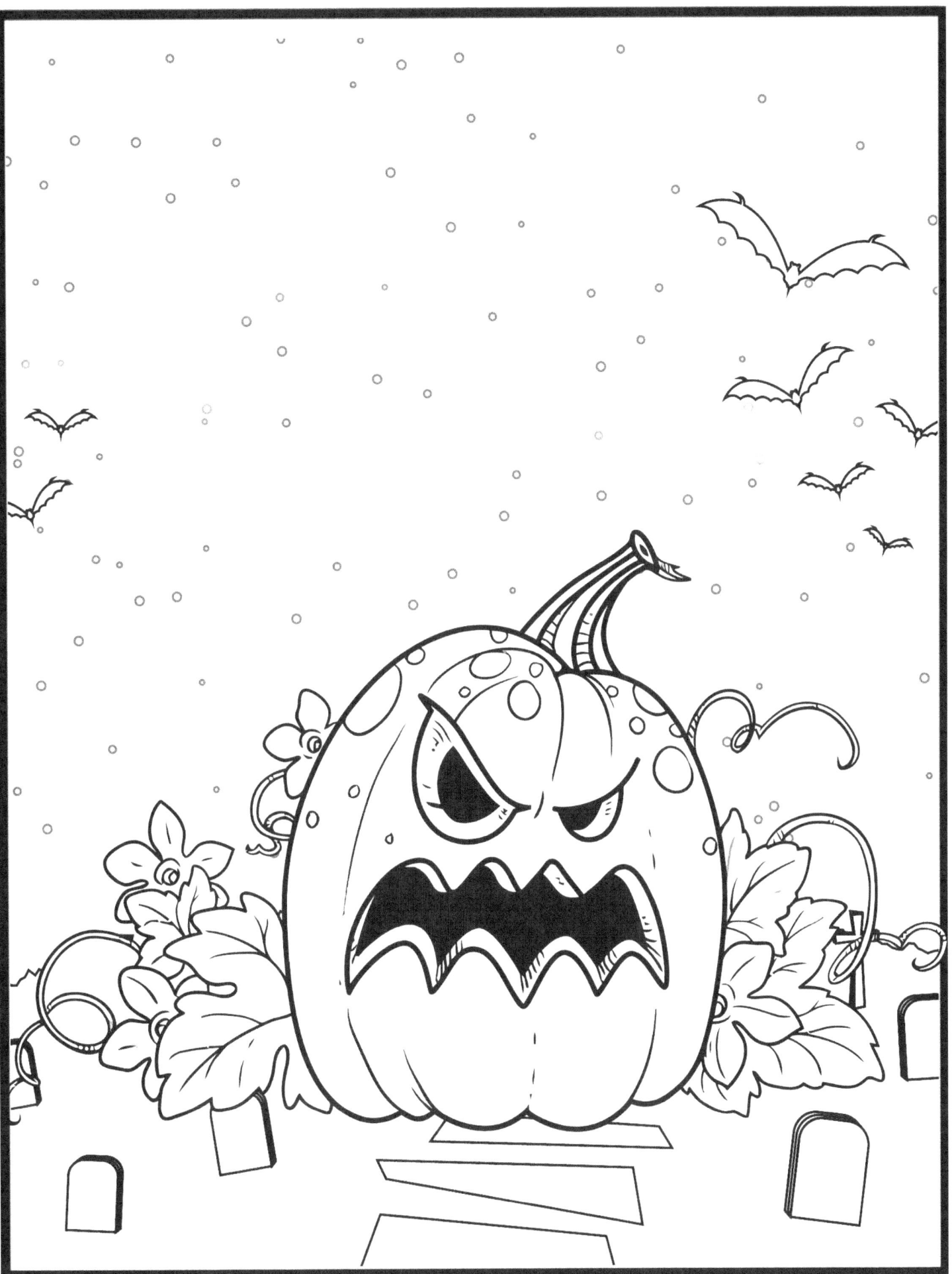

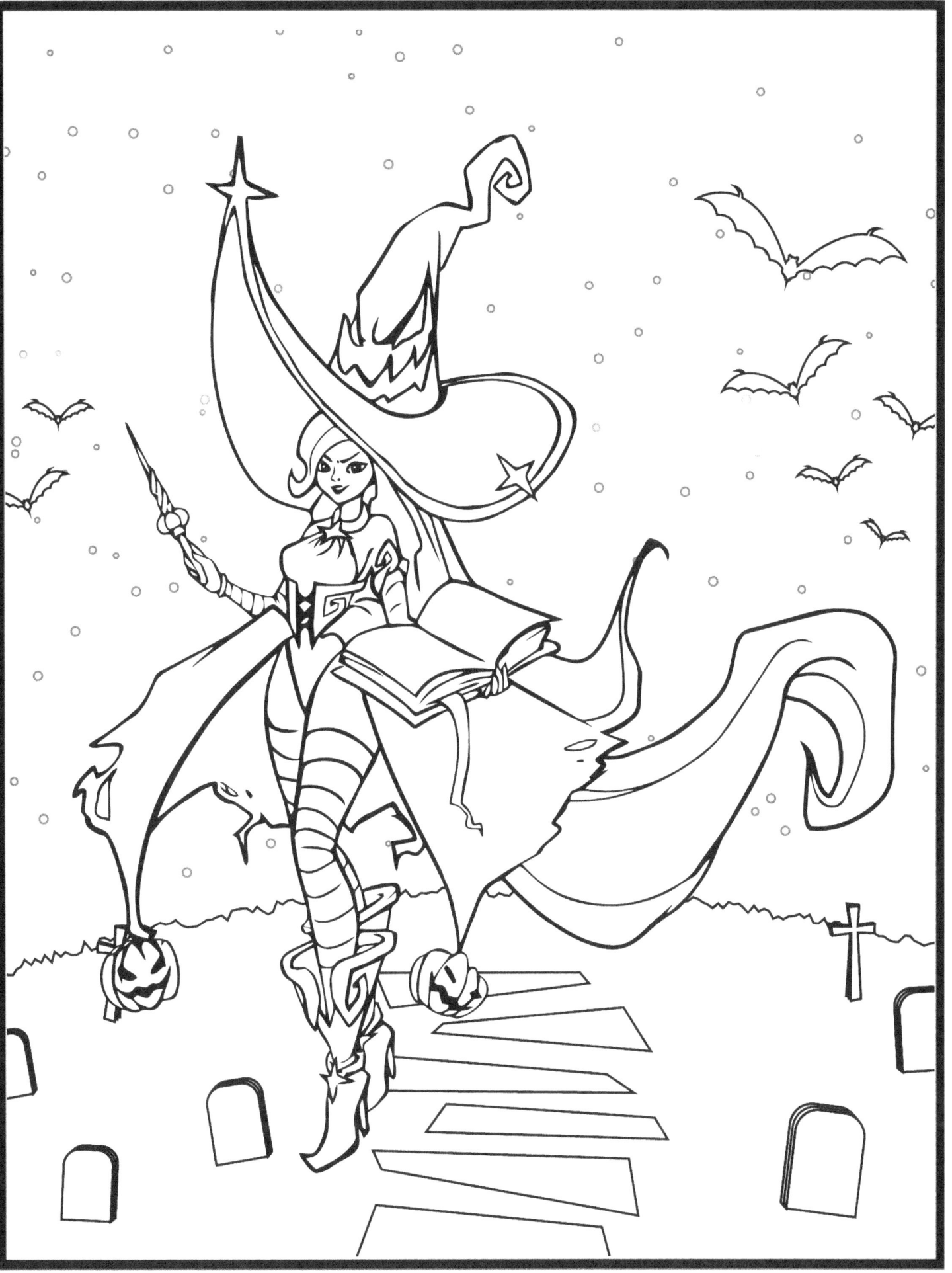

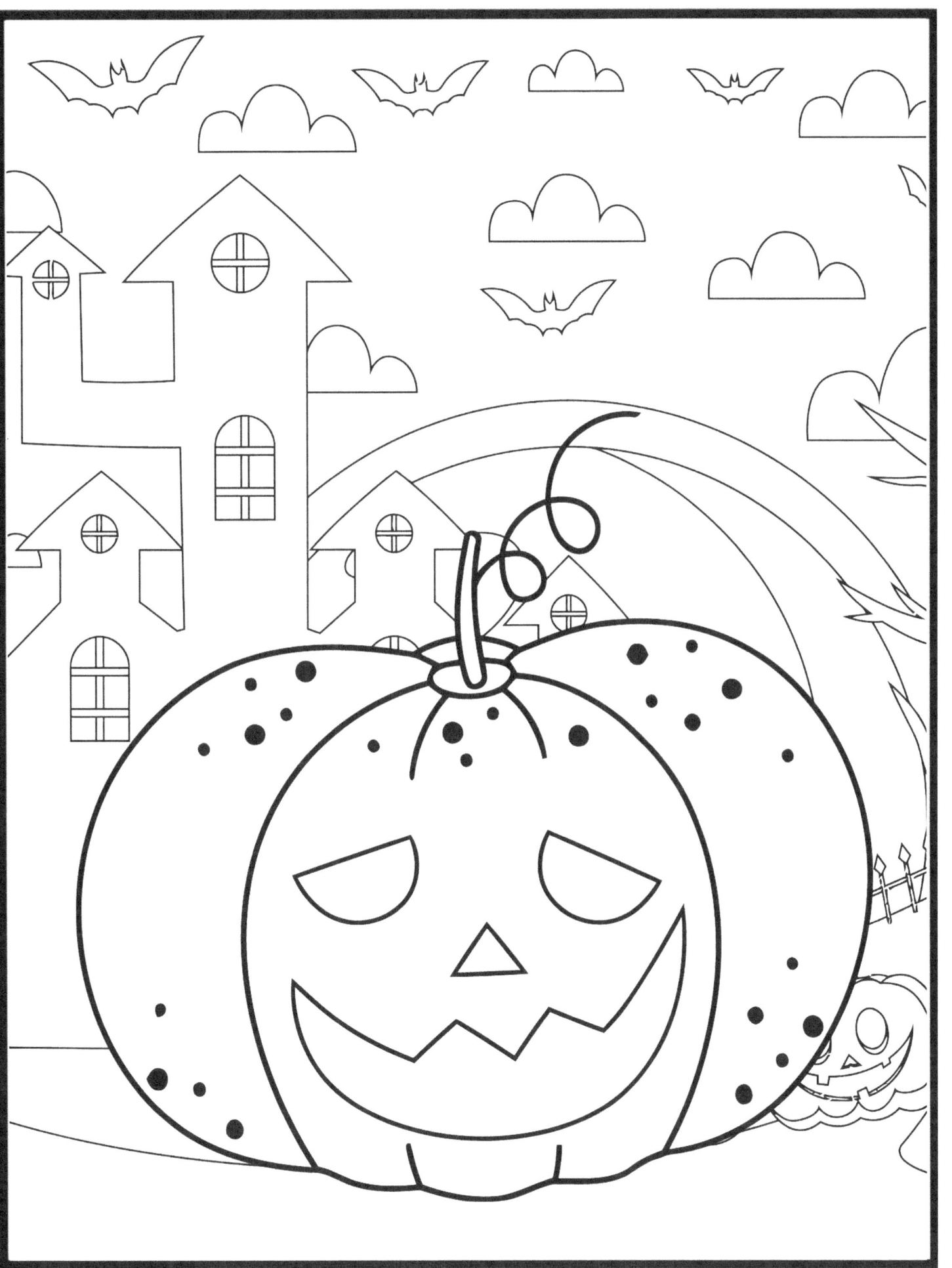

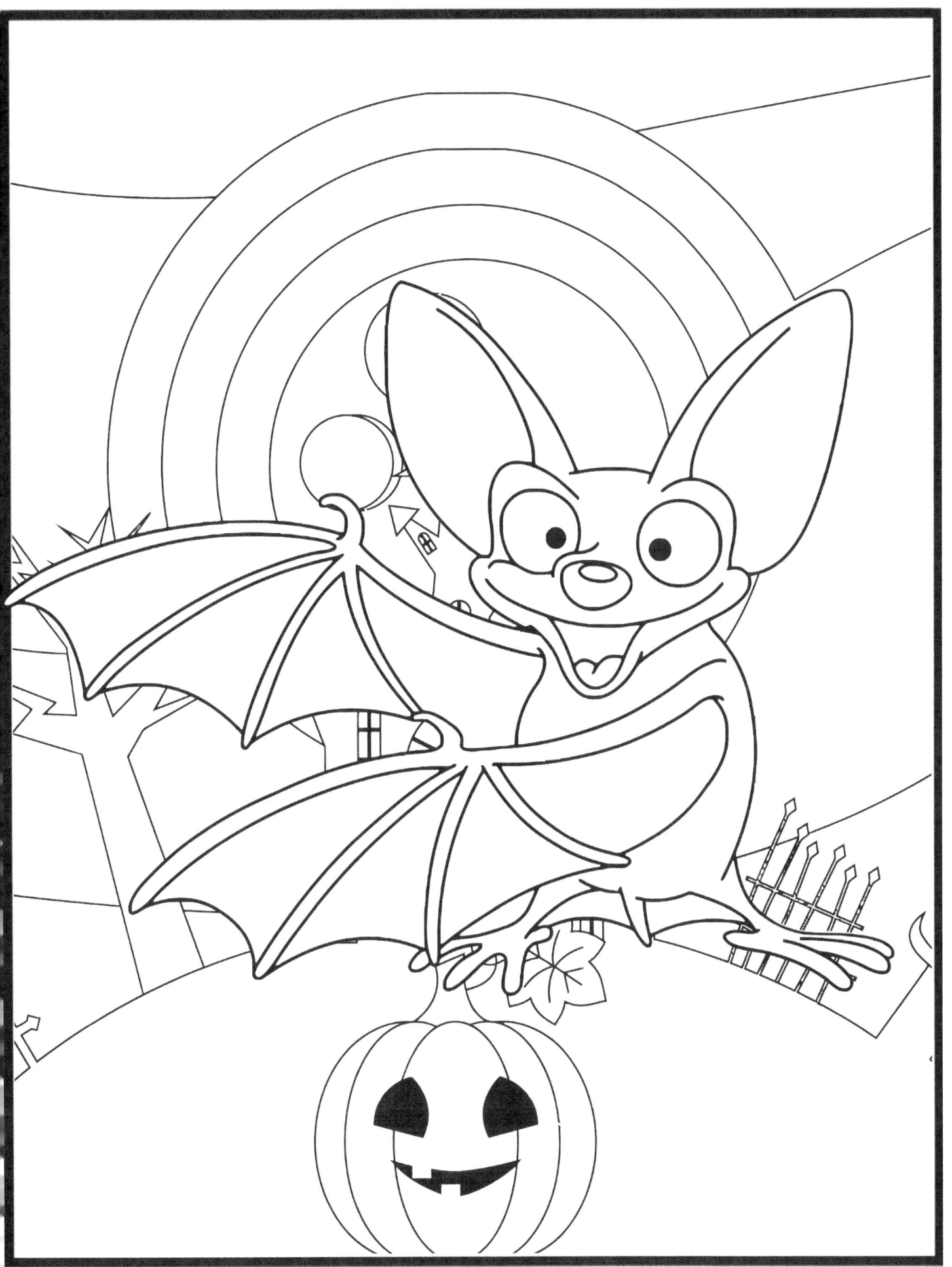

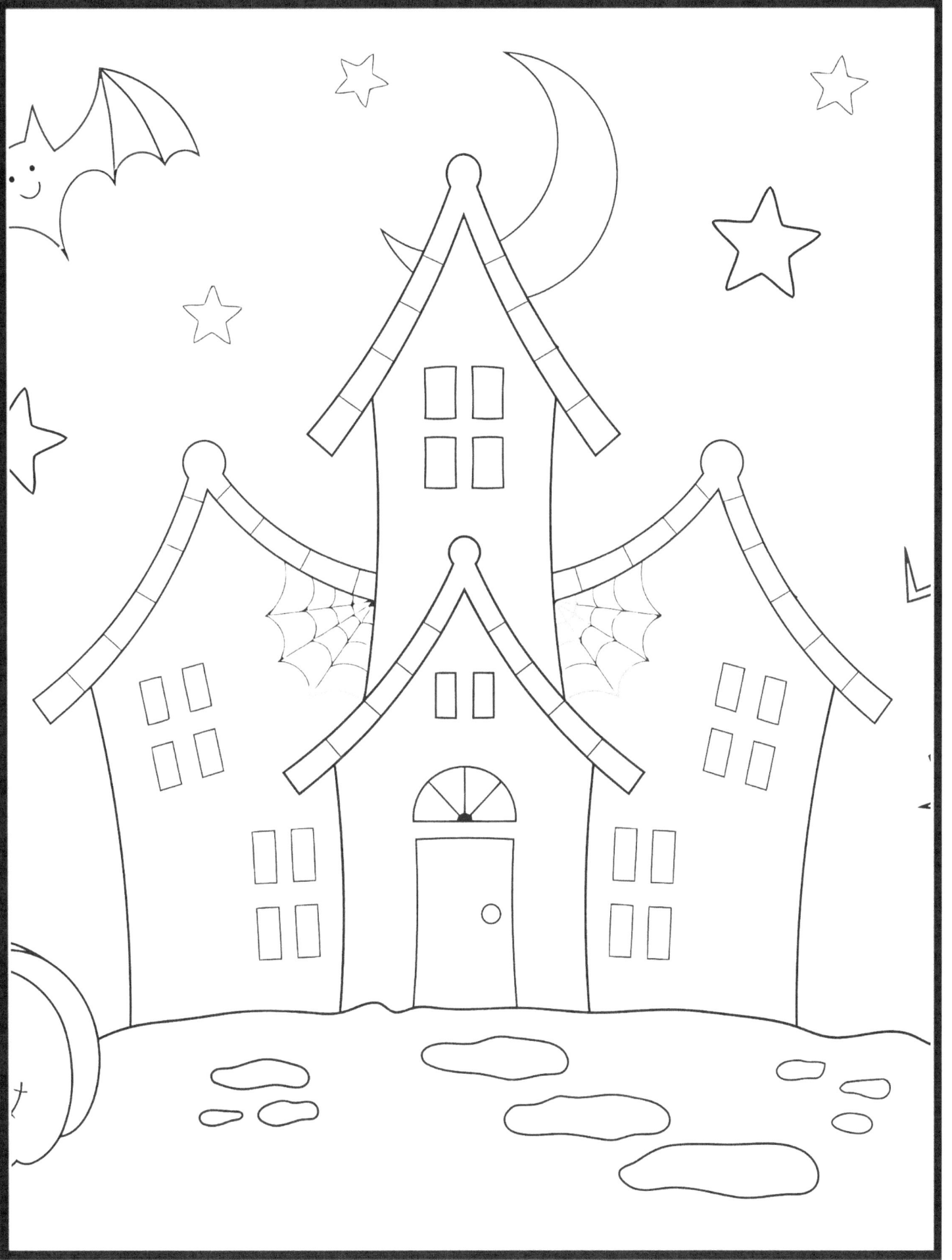

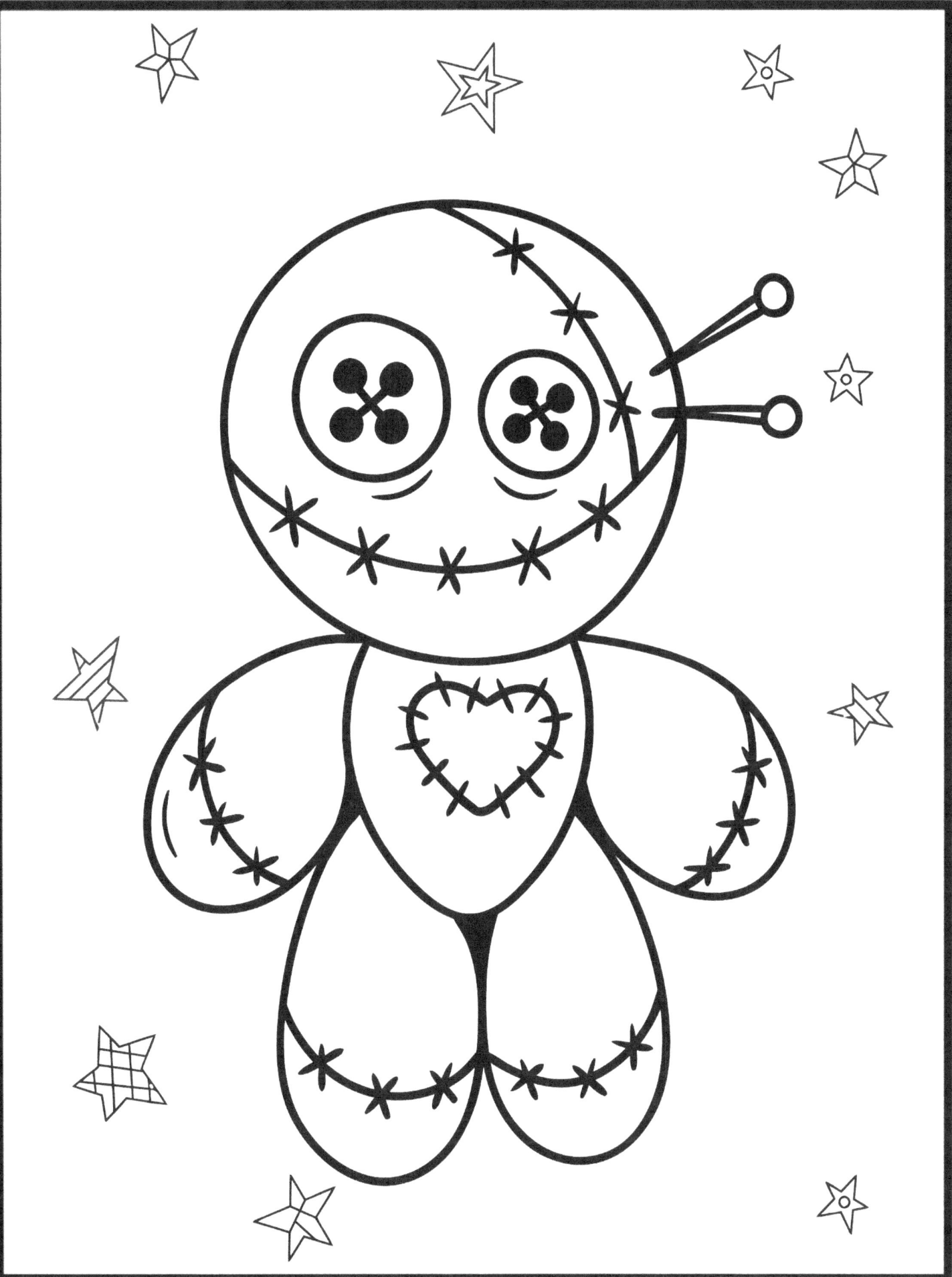

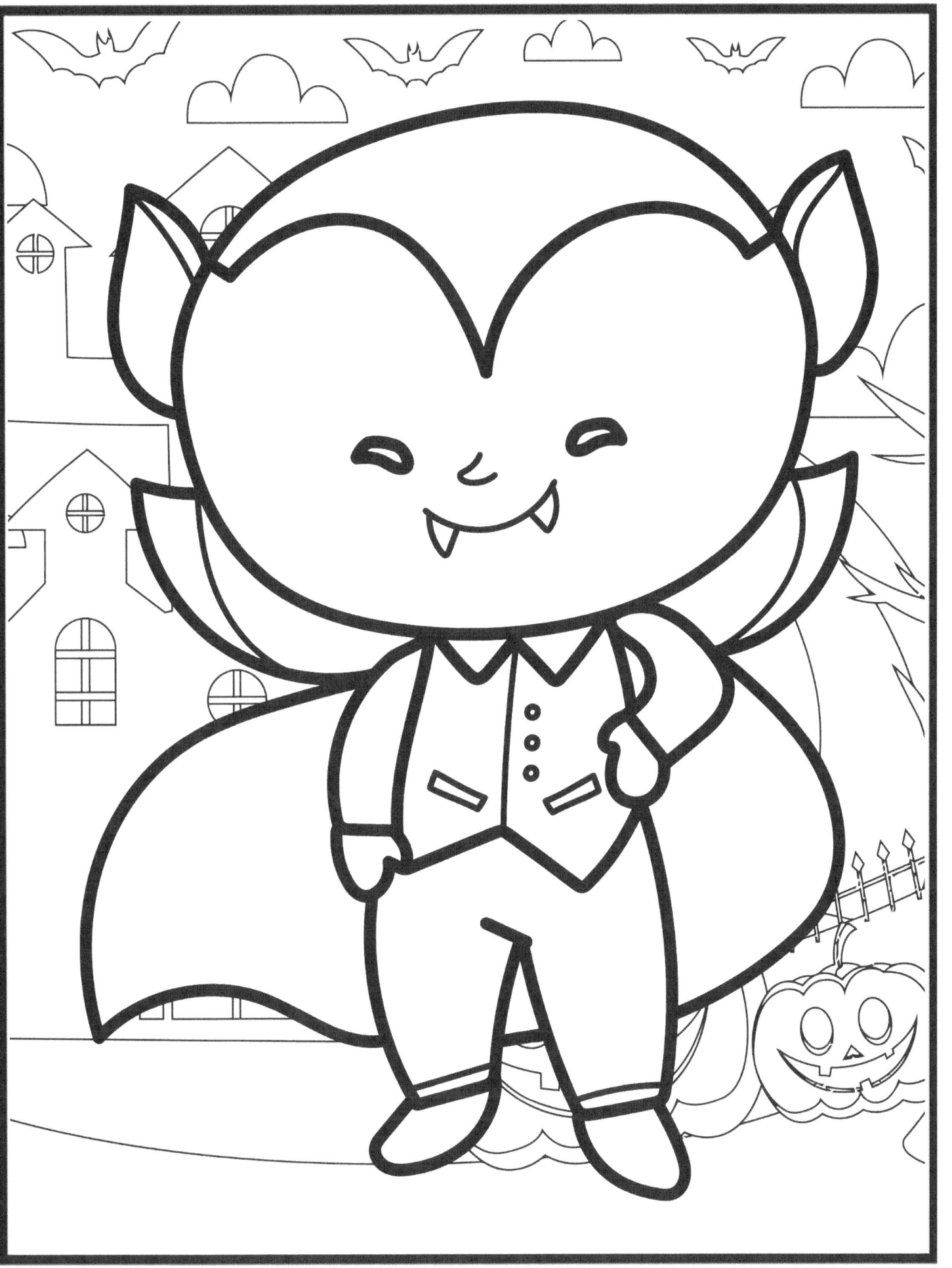

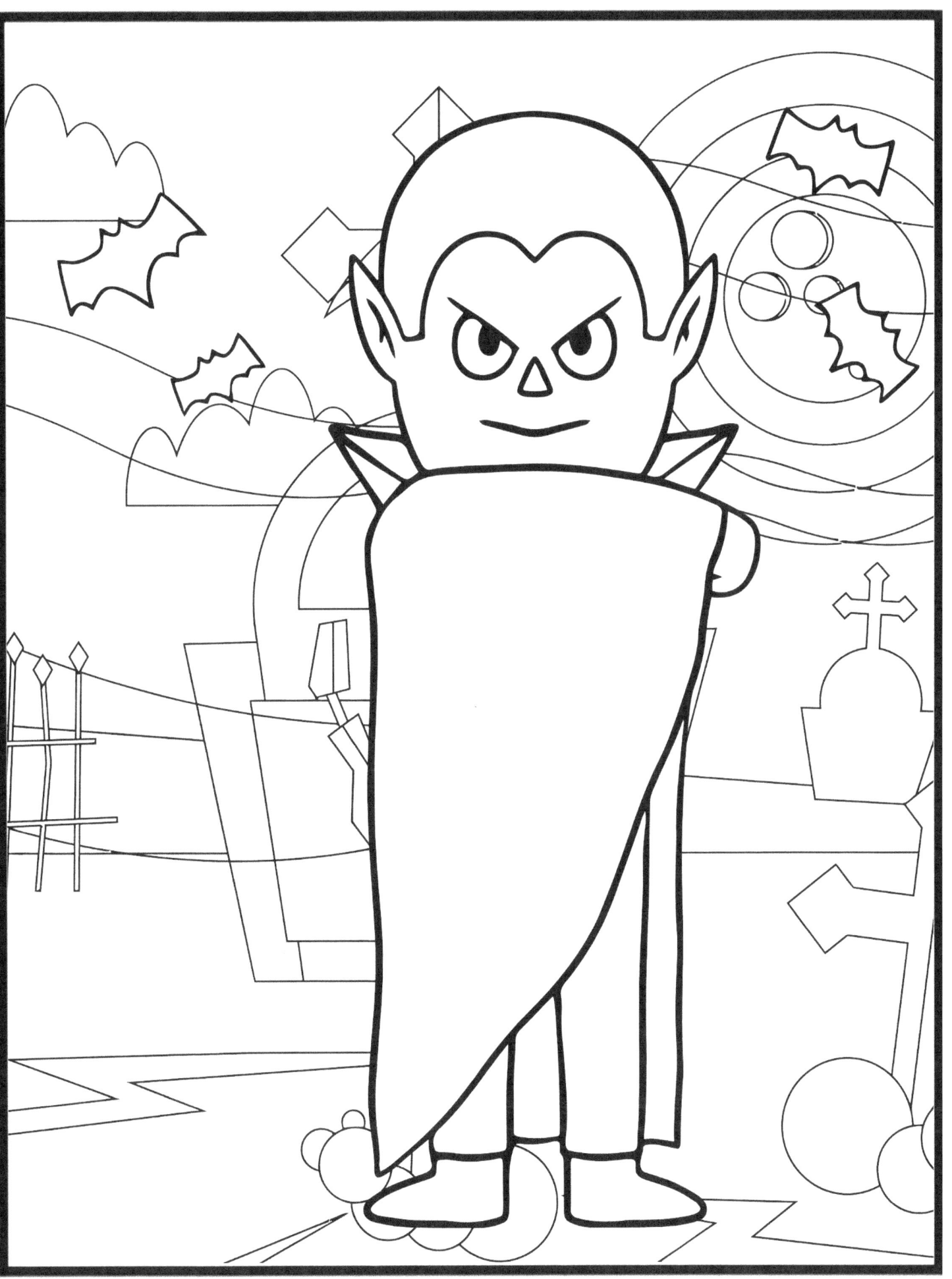

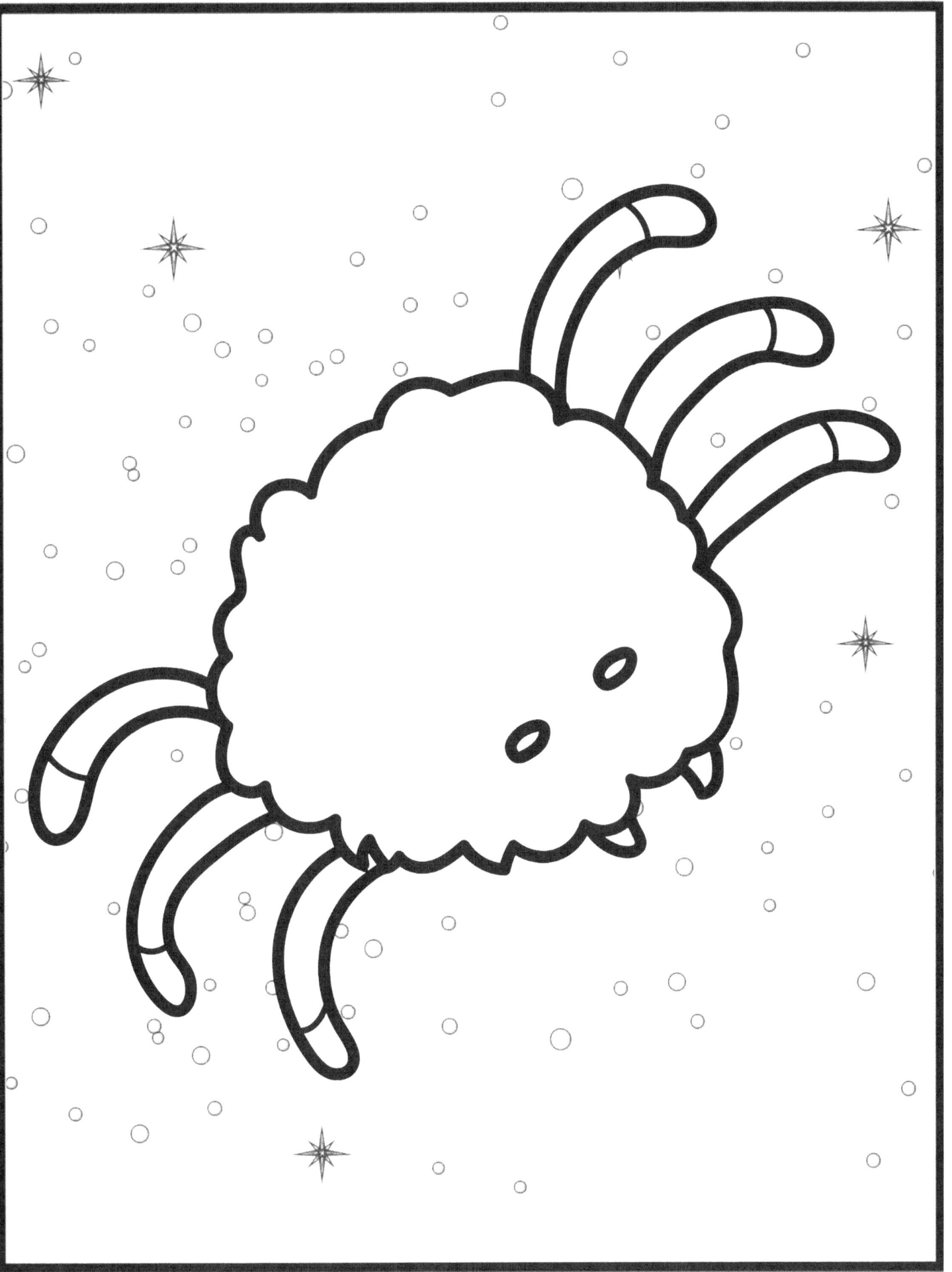

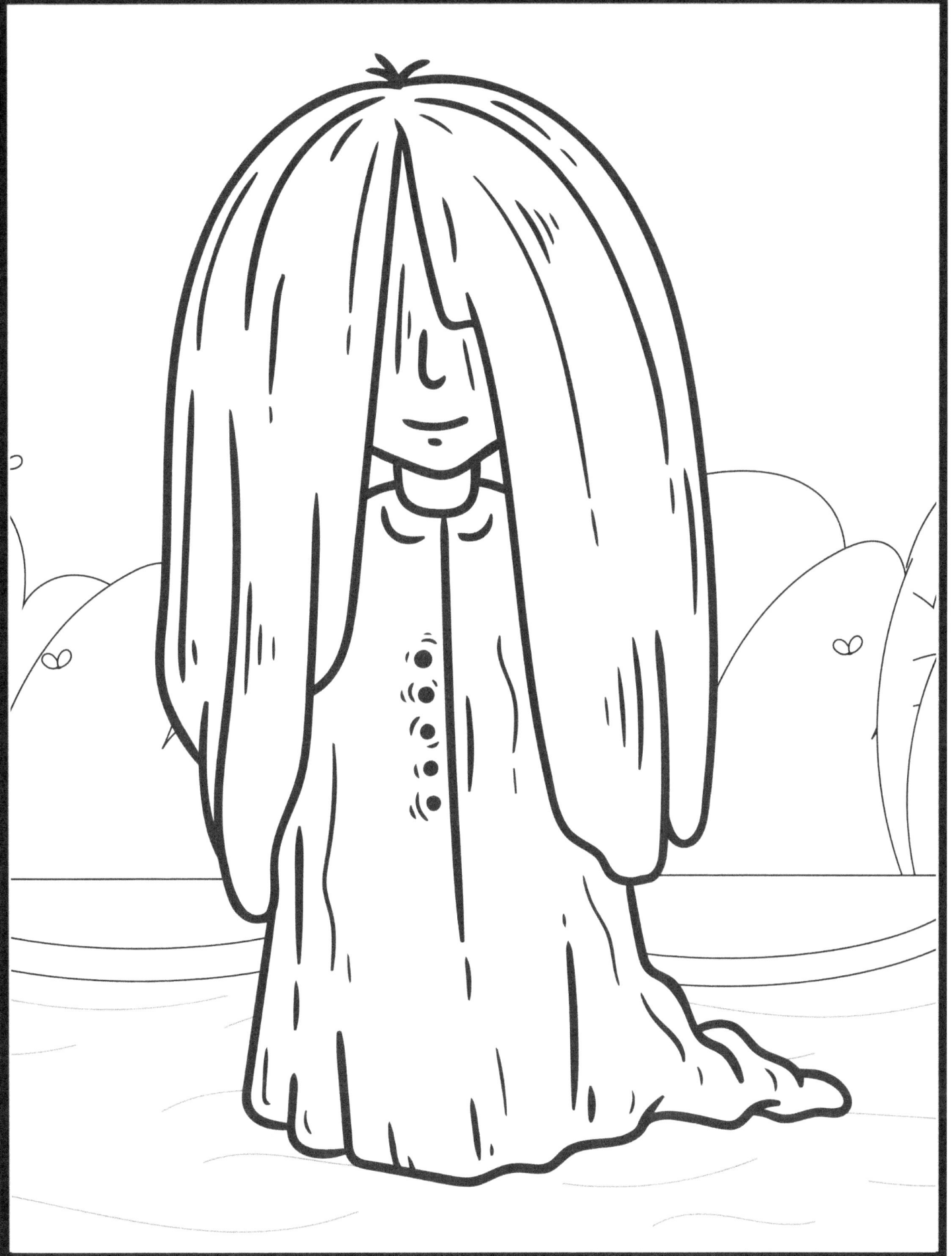

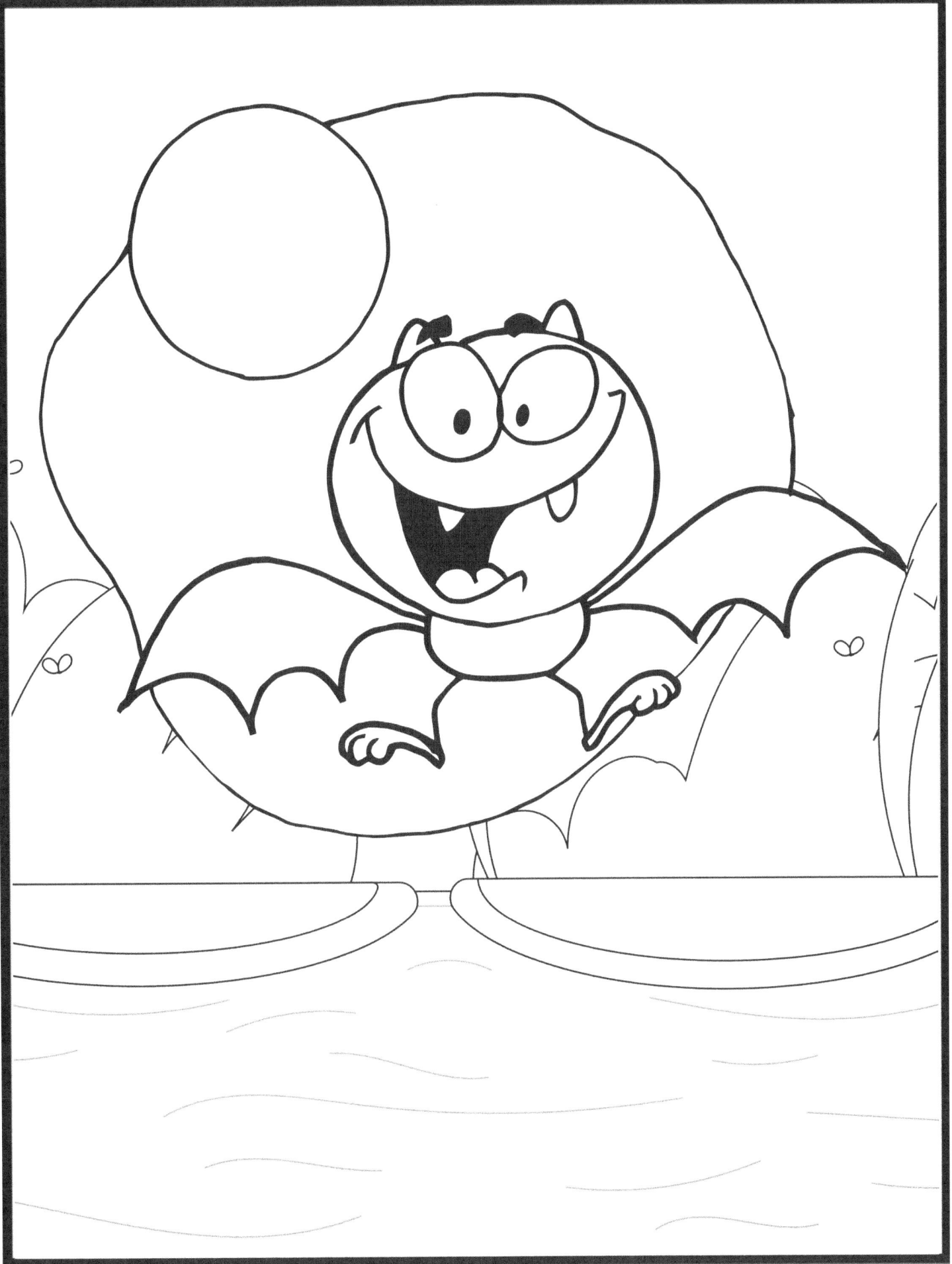

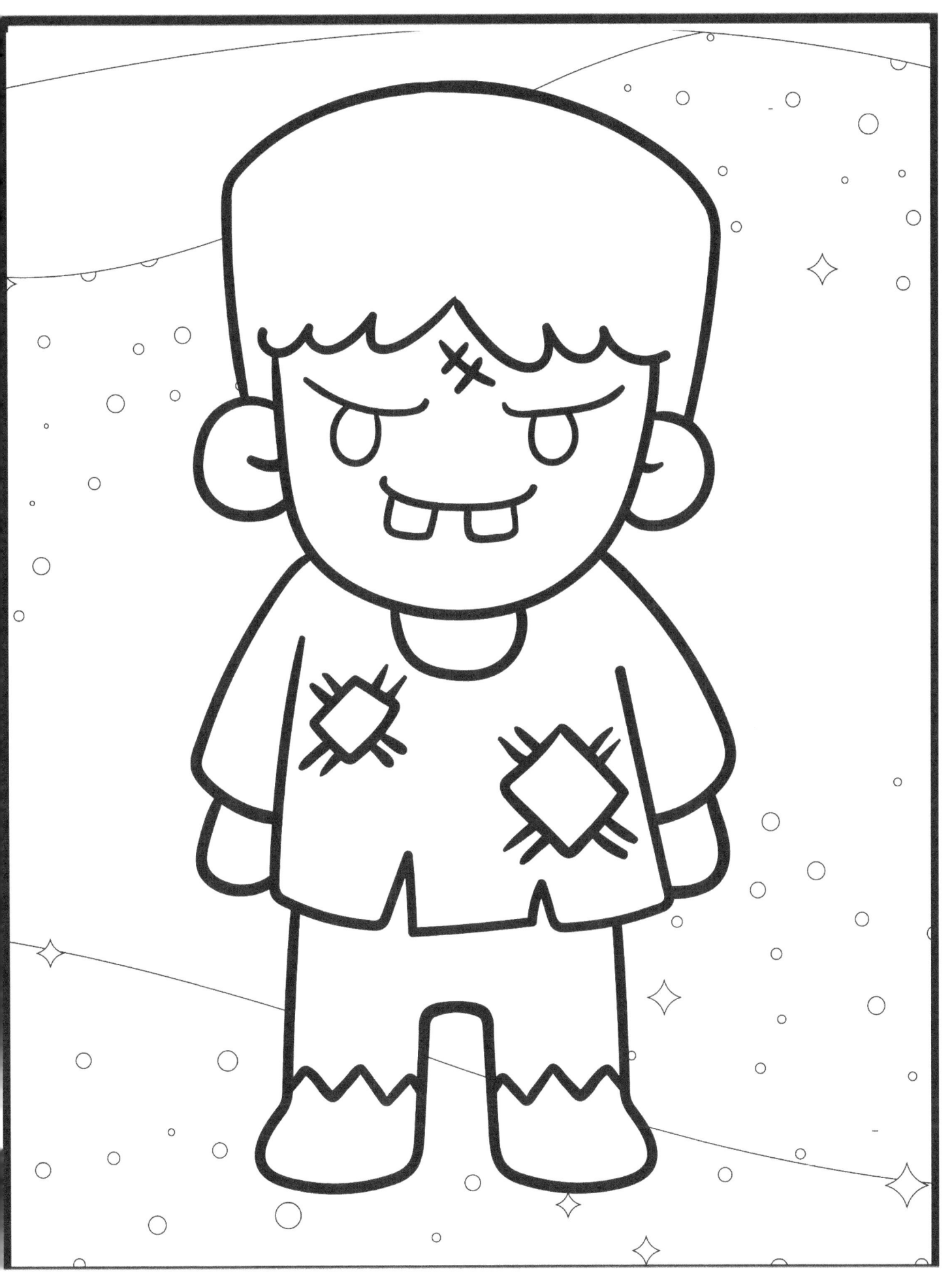

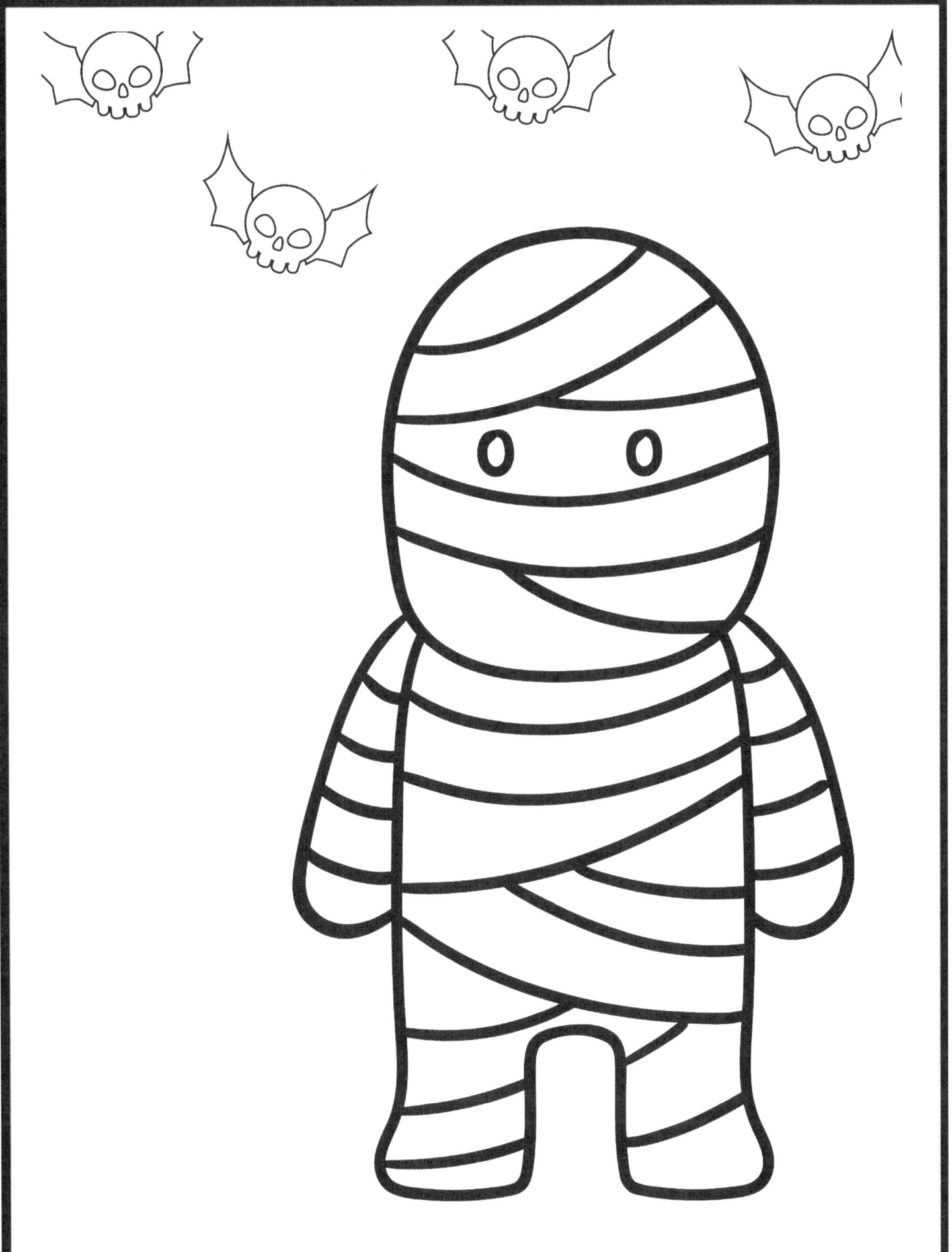

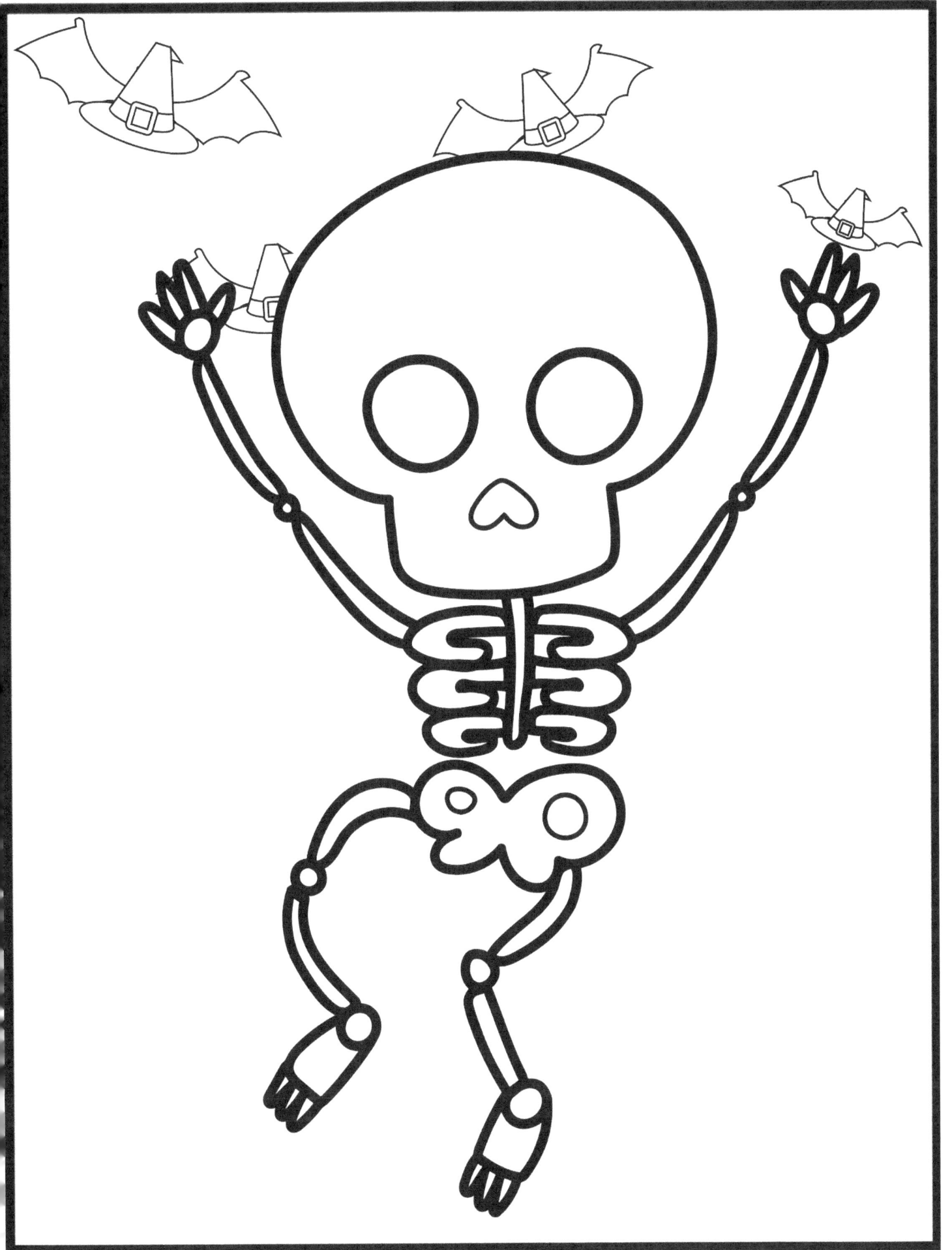

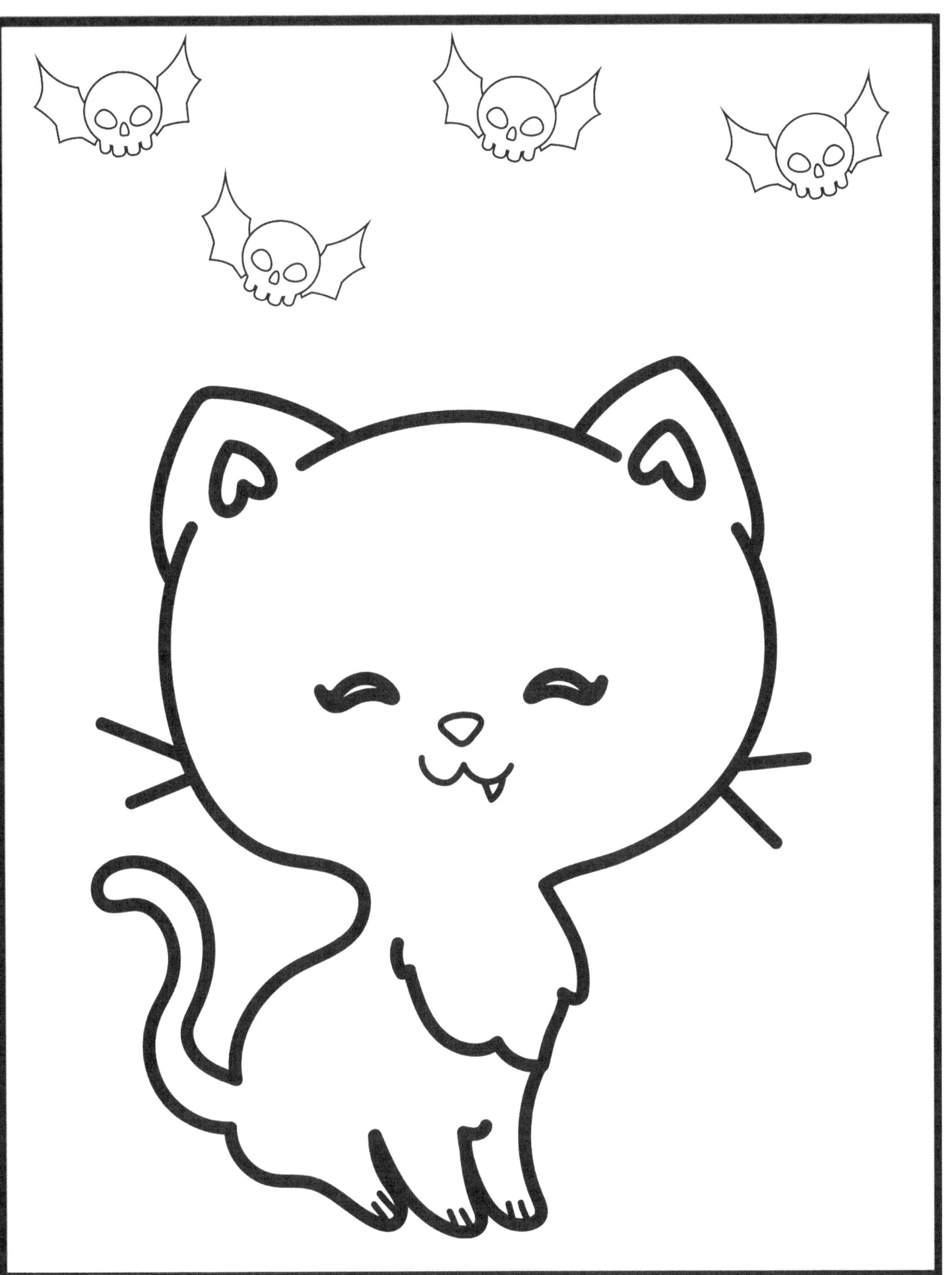

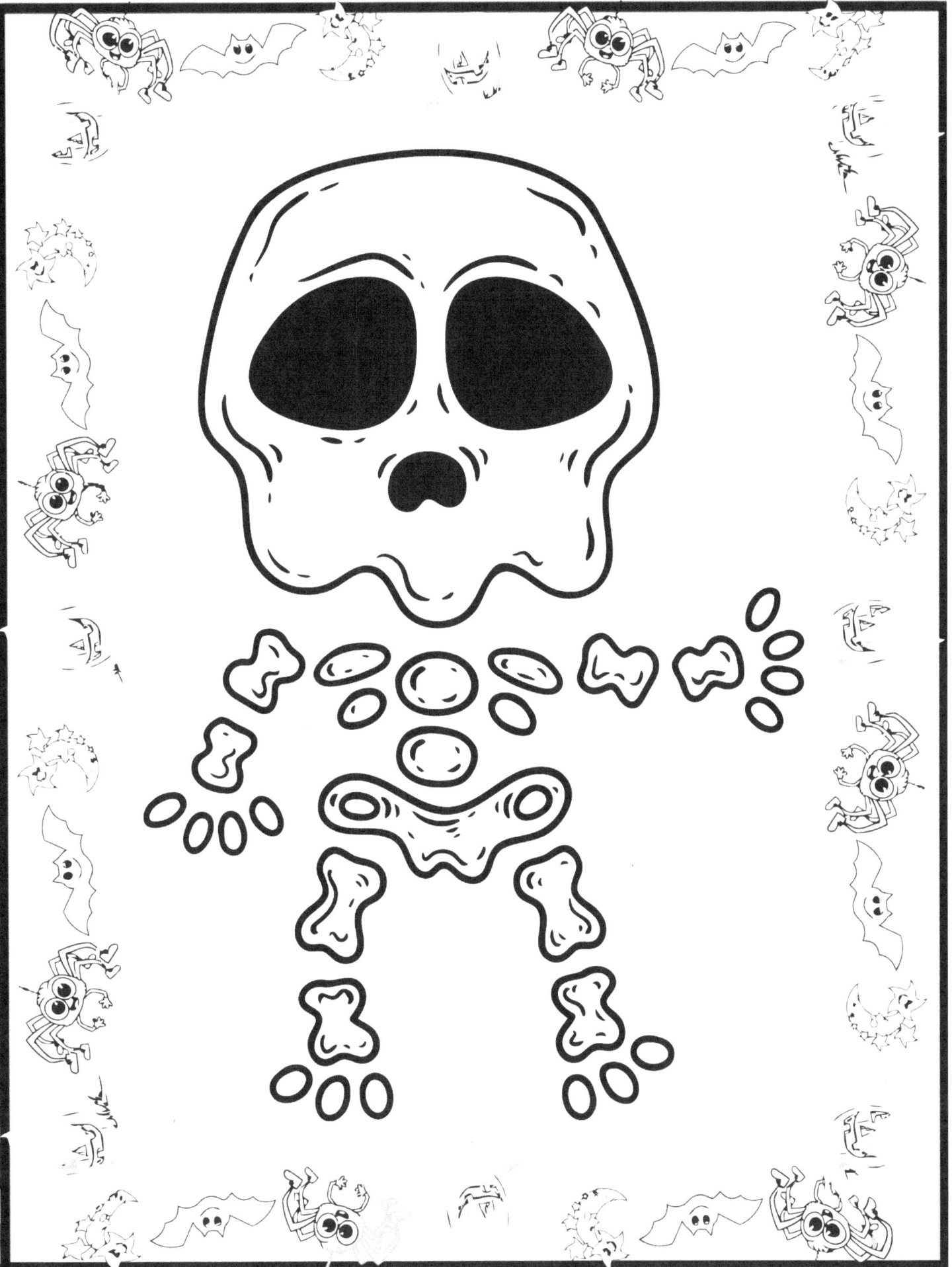

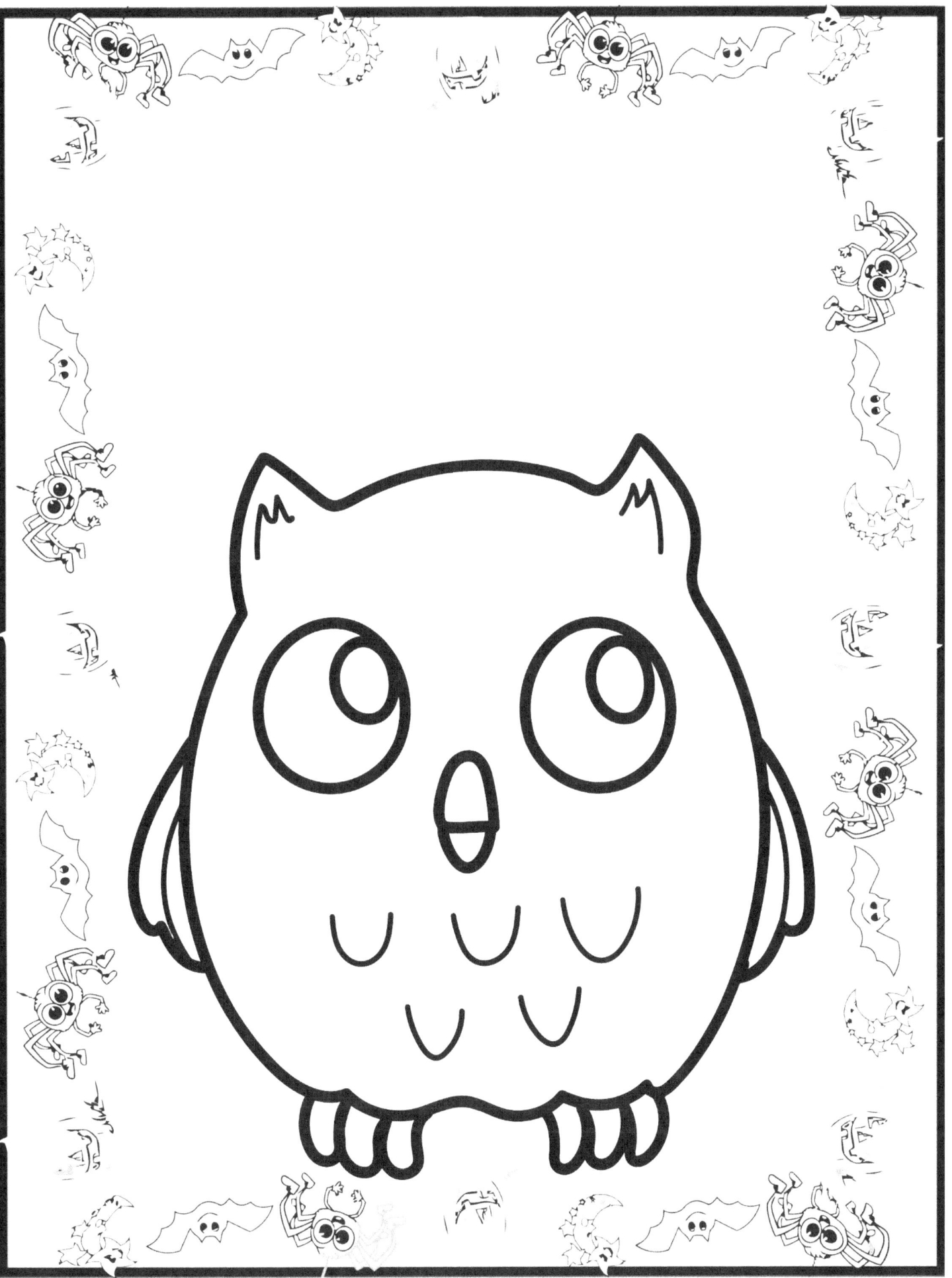

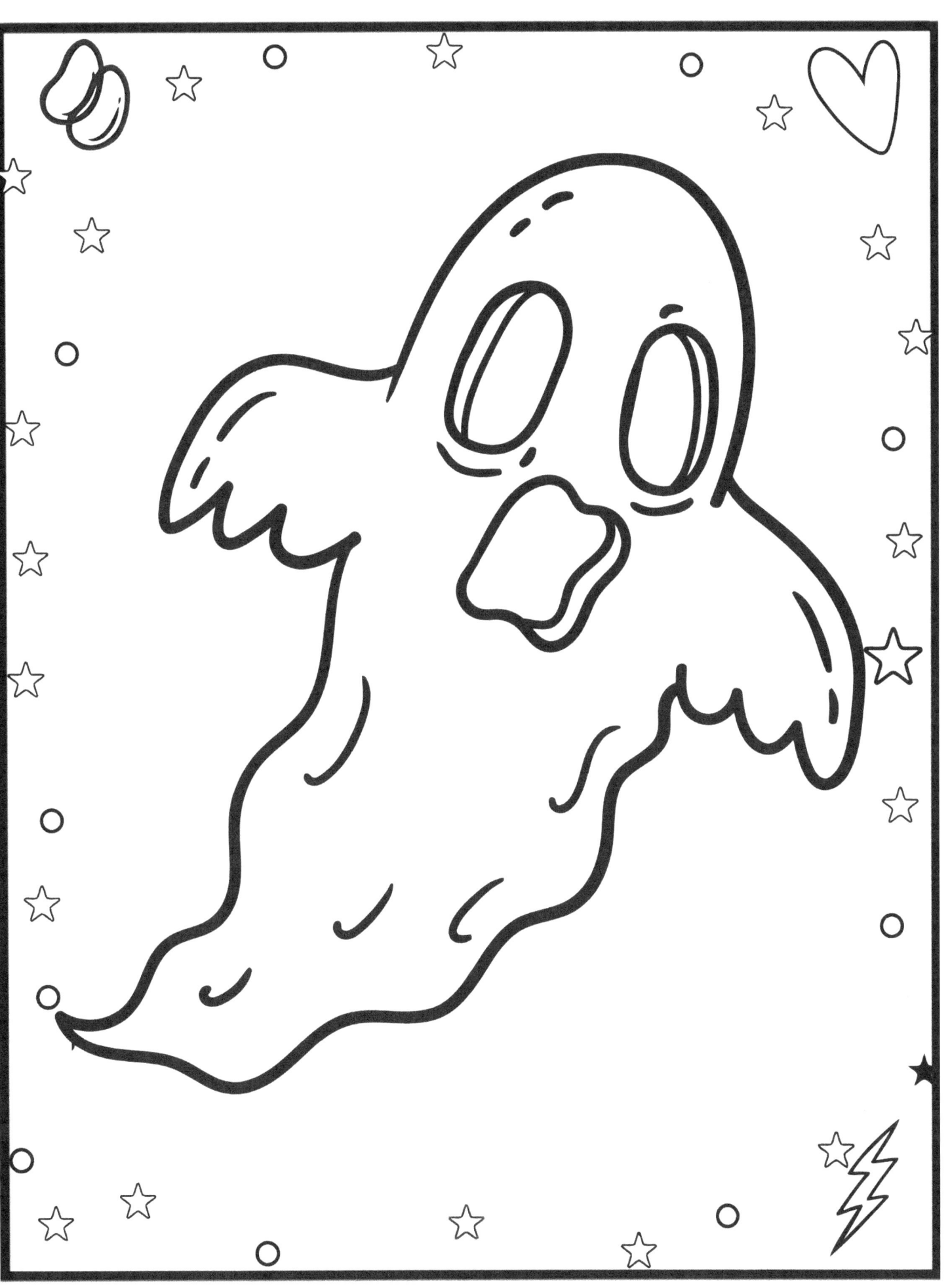

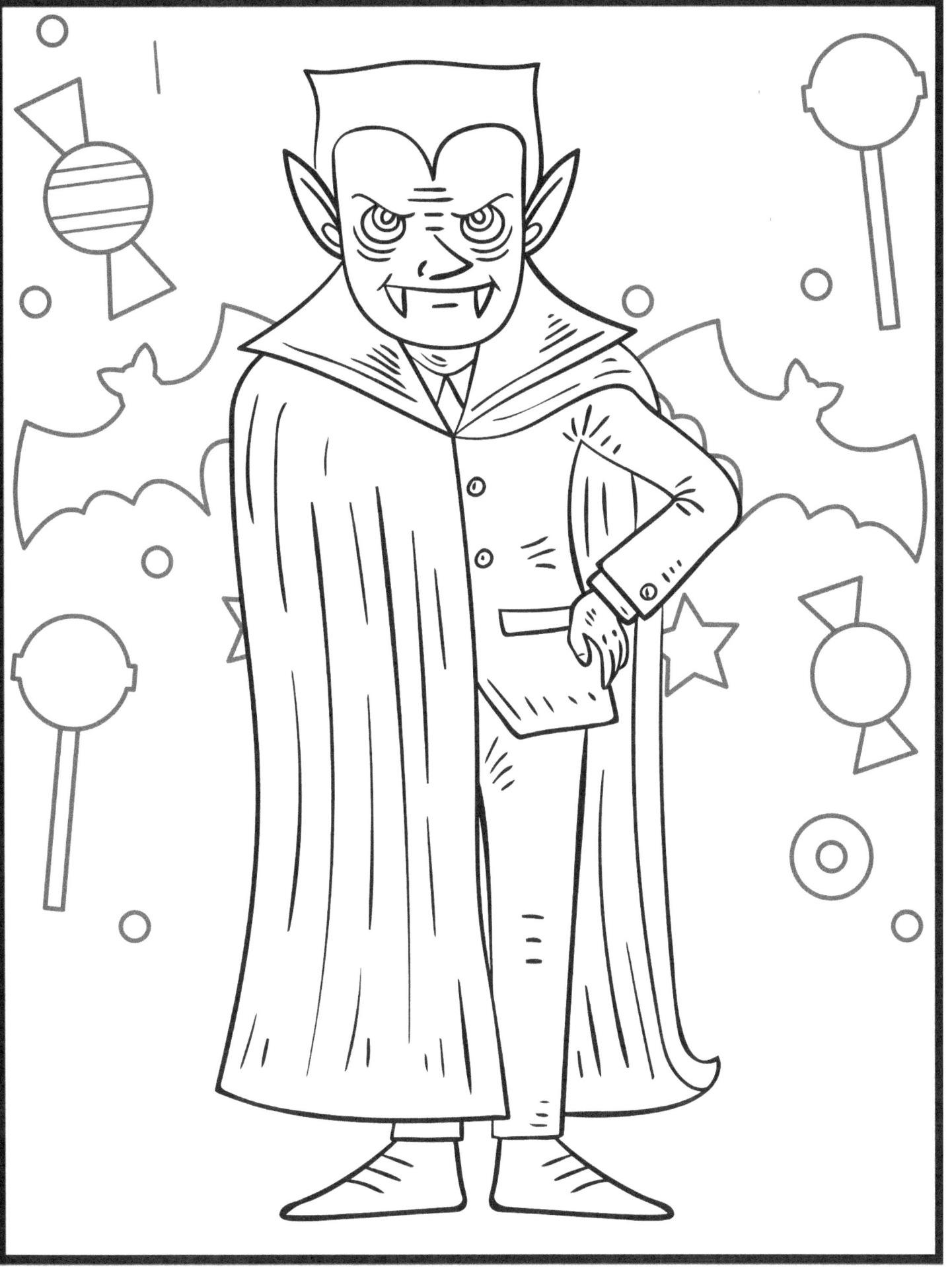

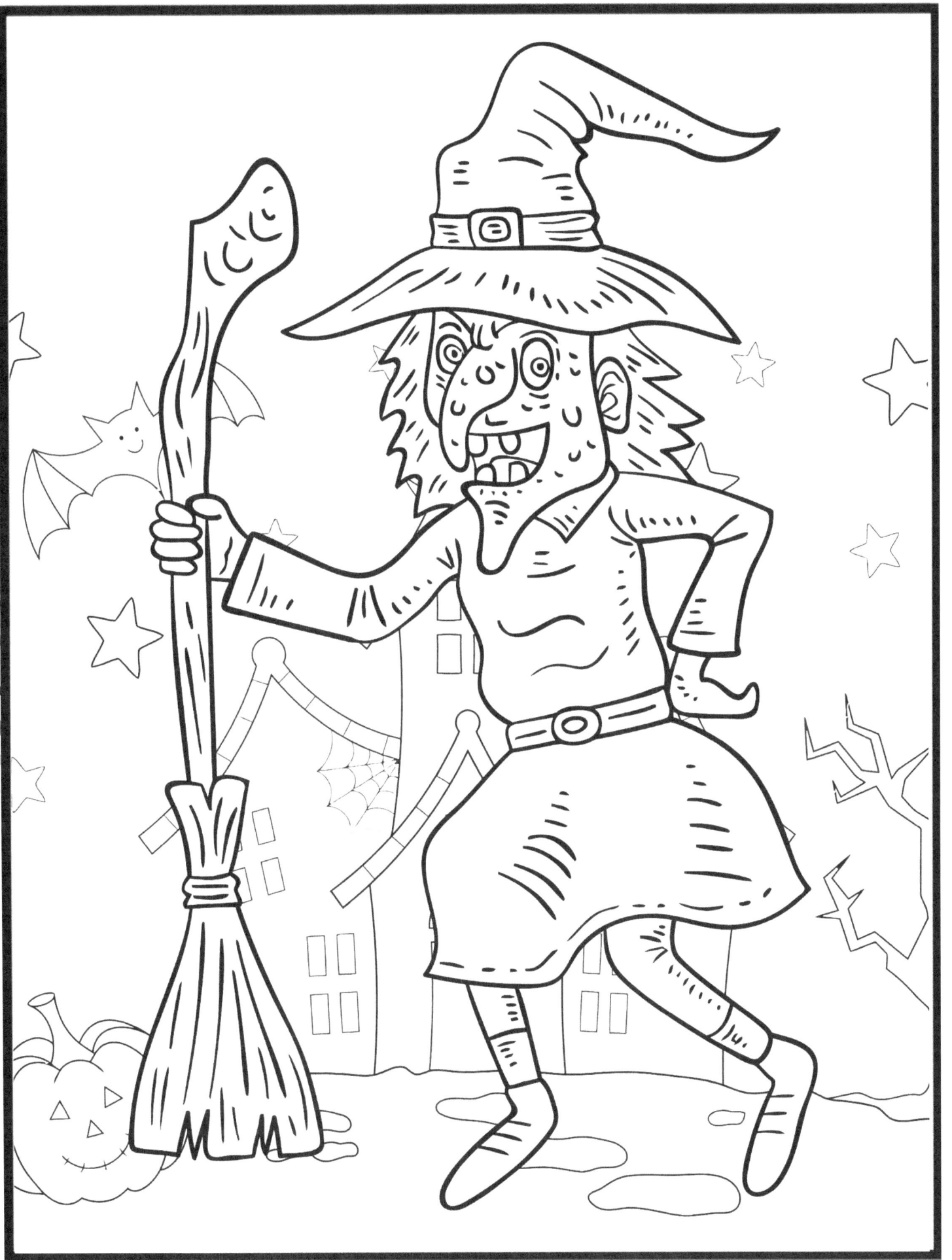

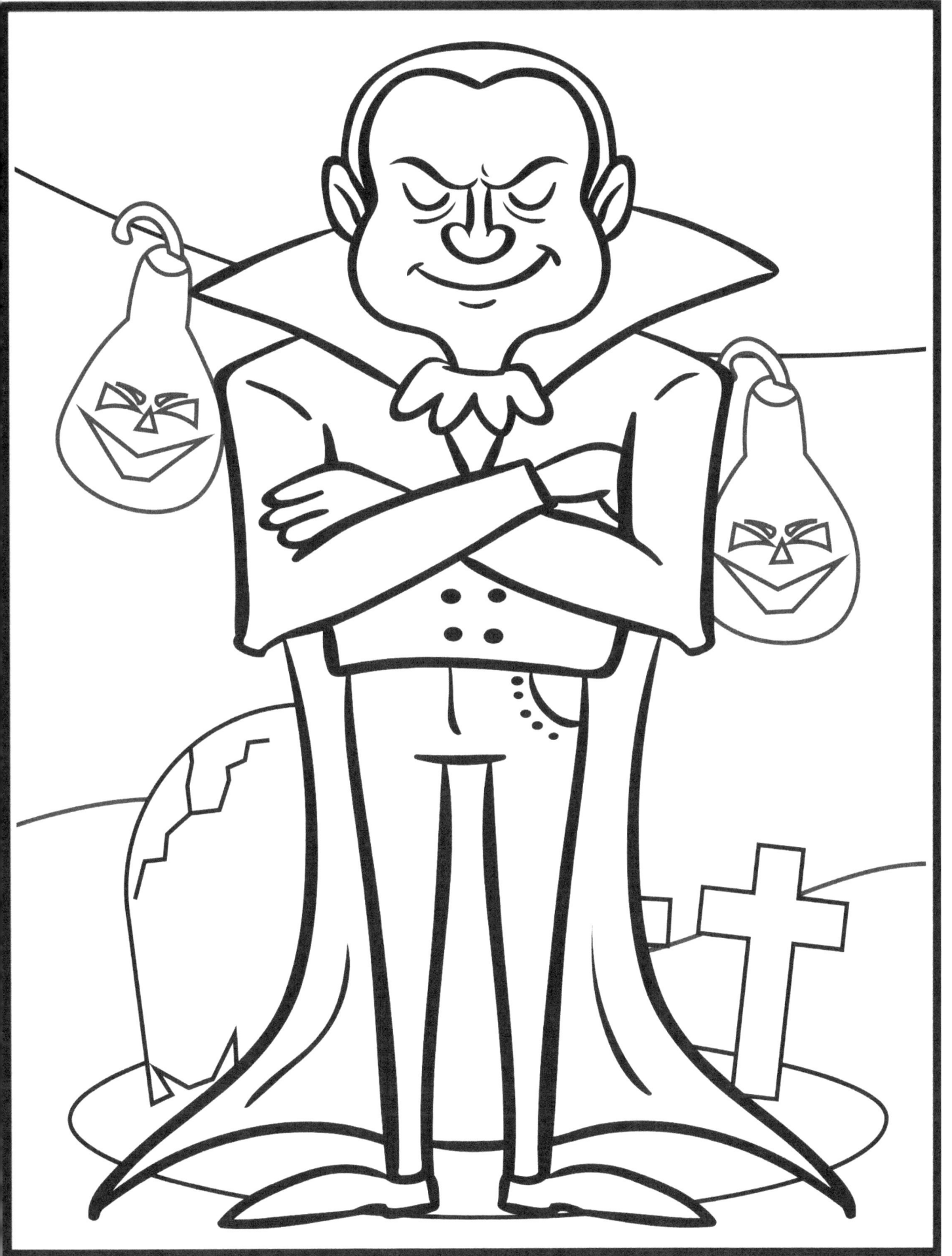

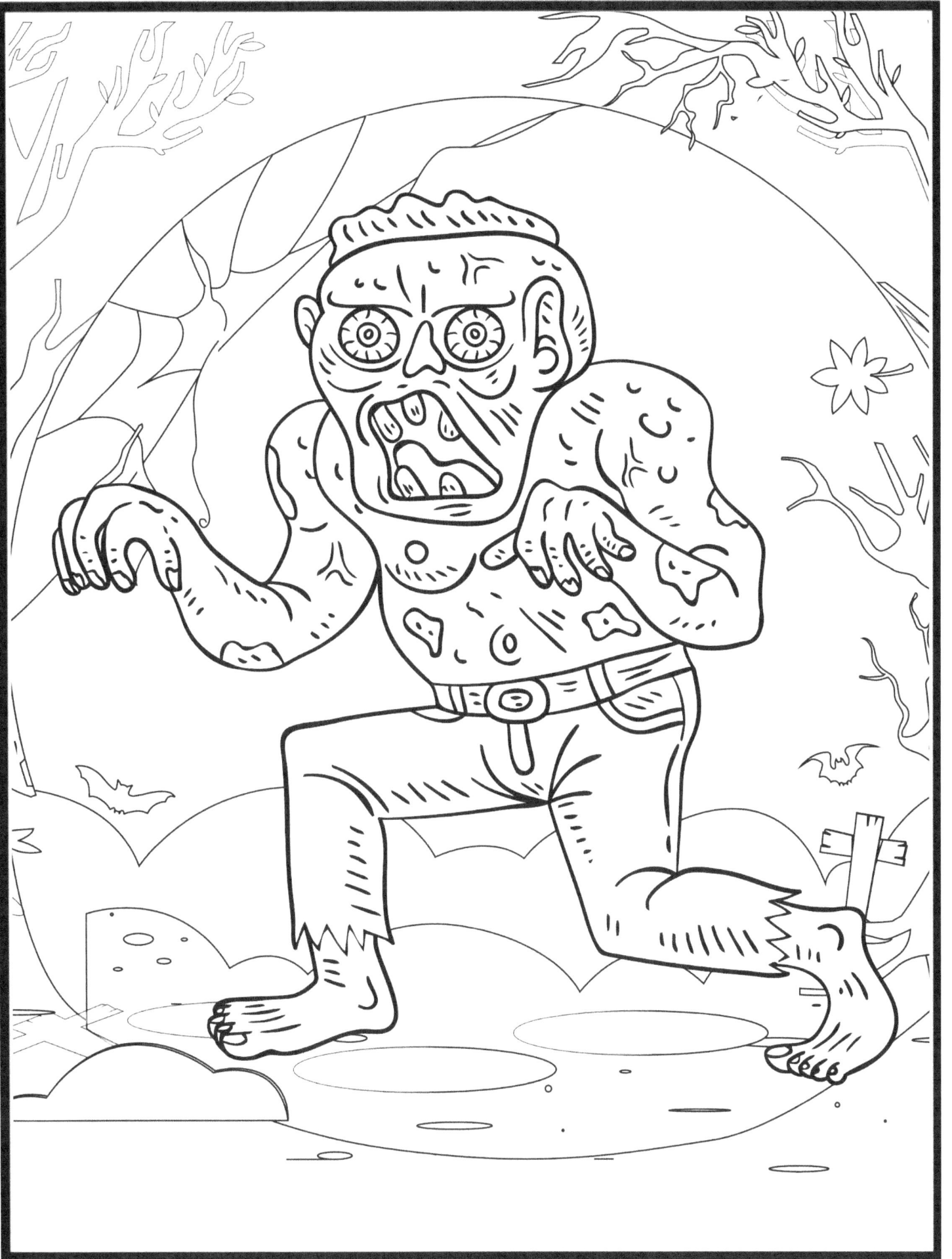

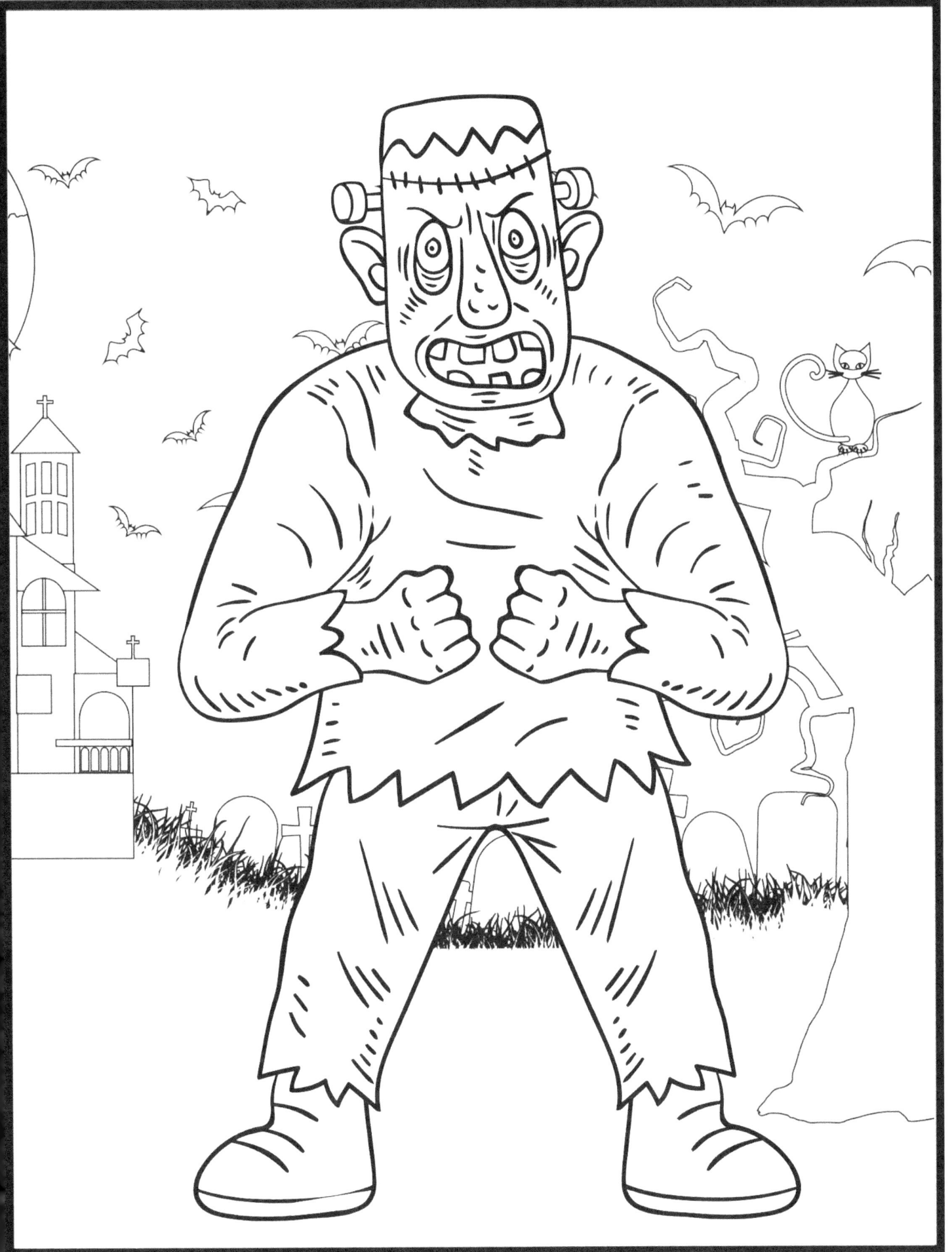

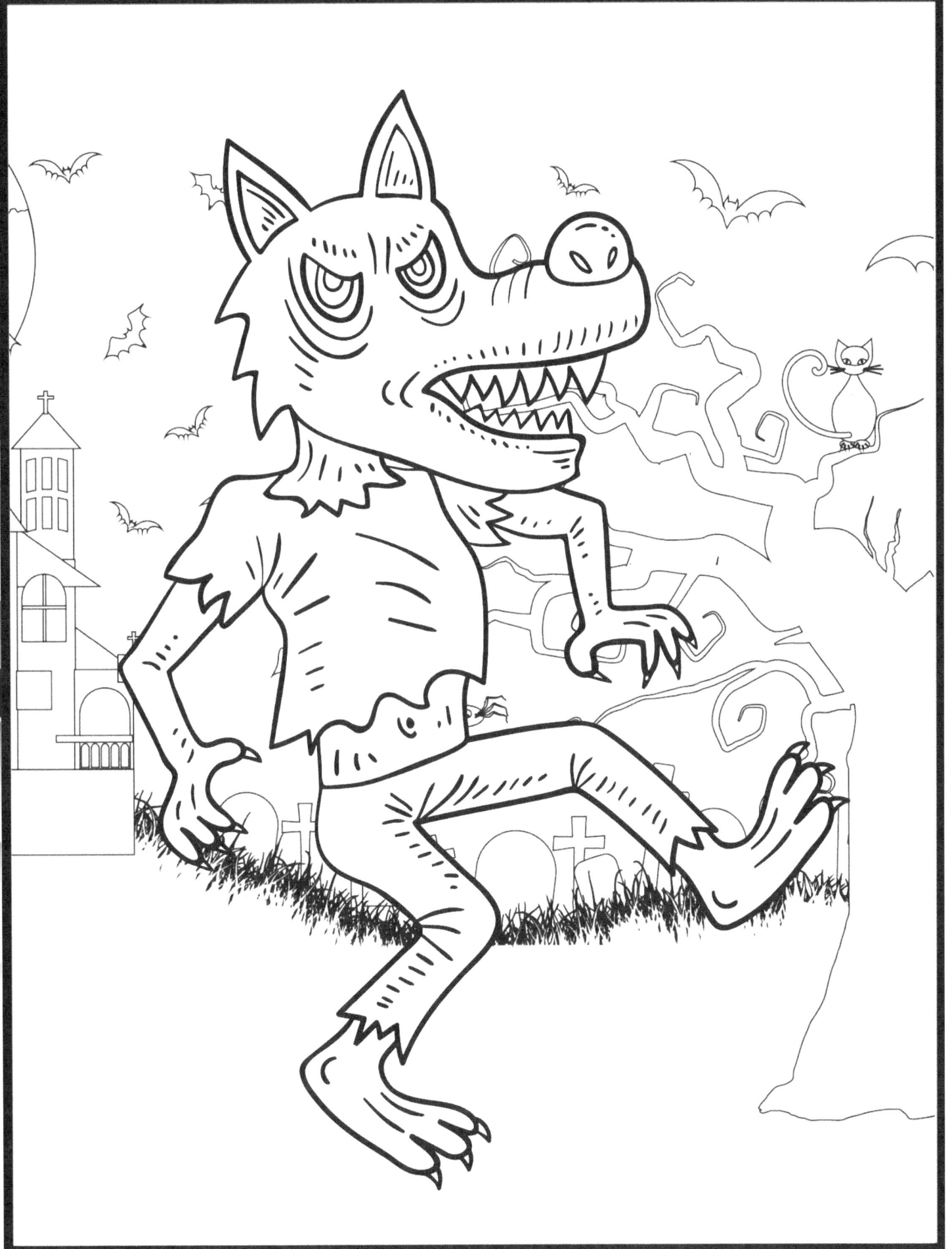

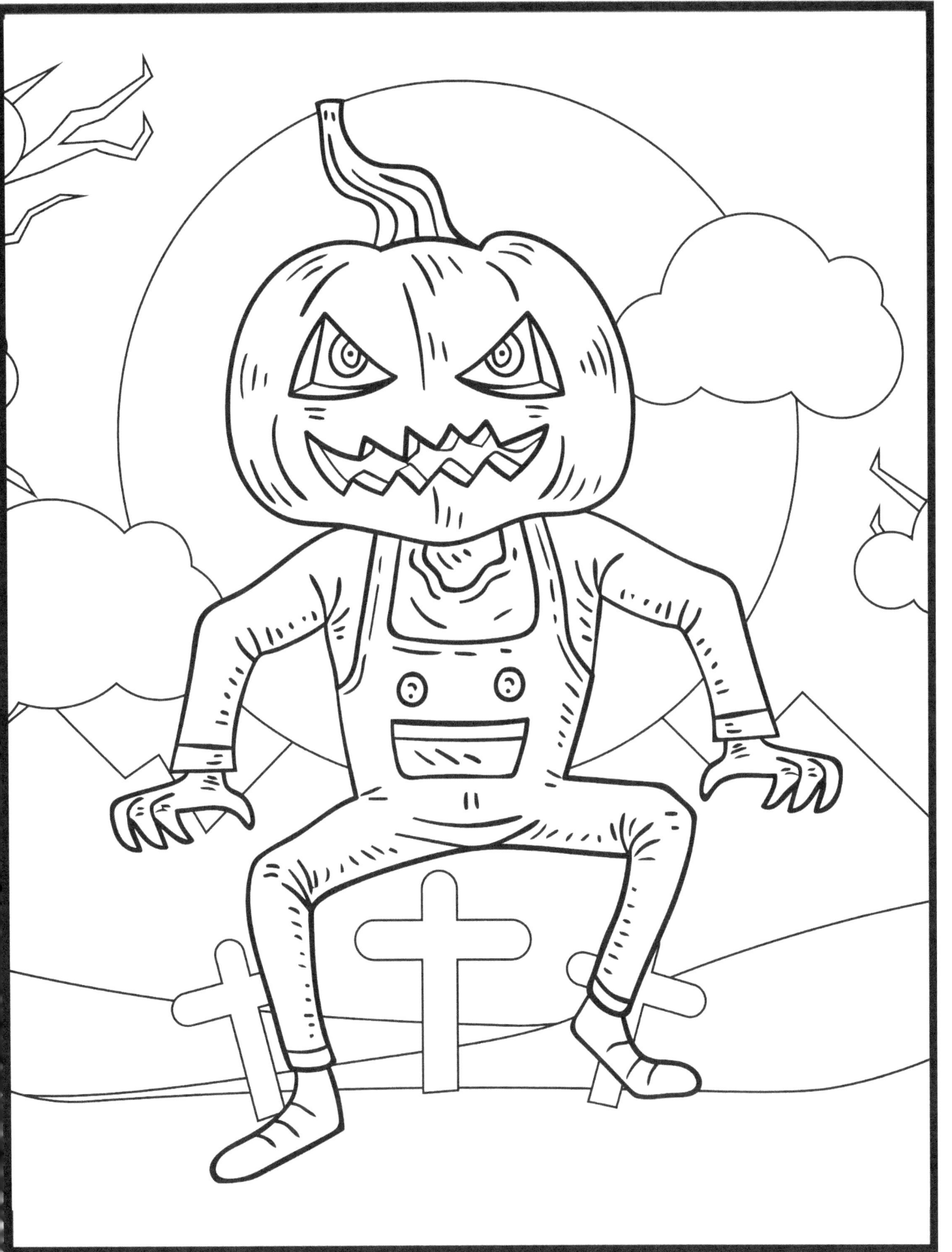

www.ingramcontent.com/pod-product-compliance
Lightning Source LLC
Chambersburg PA
CBHW060002230526
45472CB00008B/1908